How to Begin Homesteading: Start Small, Succeed, Expand!

Rachel Roy

Published by Rachel Roy Independent Publishing, 2023.

HOW TO BEGIN HOMESTEADING: START SMALL, SUCCEED, EXPAND!

First edition. June 1, 2023.

ISBN: 979-8987431429

Written by Rachel Roy.

Table of Contents

How to Begin Homesteading | Introduction to Second Time Around Homestead 1
How to begin homesteading with hardly any space and you work full time 3
Dreams 5
Some Things To Consider In Depth, Before Buying Property 11
Three lessons in the first six months that we said we really were homesteaders 20
Autumn Accountability - The First Year 27
What are your big goals for five years from now? Ten years? Retirement? 36
How To Make Money From Your Hobby Homestead 38
Message from Rachel 39
Chapter 1 - So you want to make money here, huh? 40
Chapter 2 - Your Property's Resources 48
Chapter 3 - Chickens! 50
Chapter 4 - Gardening 60
Chapter 5 - Hunting, fishing, trapping, foraging 68
Chapter 6 - Make money with your hobby 78
Our Homestead's Recipes 88
Tips and Tricks 89
Slow Cooker 91
Casseroles 99
Other meals that don't have a category... 109
Baked goods 117
Cook ahead and portion for microwave meals 122
Seafood 131
Too Many Eggs! 136
Desserts 142
Dehydrator 151
Preserves & pickles 158

How to Begin Homesteading

Introduction to Second Time Around Homestead

Who we are and why we know what we are talking about

Rachel has grown up and lived most of her life in the rural area of the Northeast Kingdom of Vermont. This rugged landscape raises hardworking, independent people and Rachel is no different. Her husband, Chris, is a millwright and fabricator. He works both as a self-employed business owner and for other companies depending on his mood. Rachel teaches Humanities and freelance writes while running their hobby homestead. Four children and their extra curricular activities spread across four schools (middle school to college) have kept the family busy. Their children have grown up exploring the woods and mountains while immersed in the family tasks of animals and gardening since they were born, just as Rachel and Chris were. Likewise, they are all pretty proficient at baking and grilling.

Everyone pitches in whether it be gardening, splitting/hauling/stacking firewood, taking care of animals, maple sugaring, or just general tasks around the homestead.

During warmer weather you may find Rachel at local farmers markets sharing her tasty pickles or fruit spreads, fresh vegetables, and a wide variety of crafts such as her signature eco-friendly, grain bag totes. Always eager to meet new people in the Kingdom, Rachel loves sharing tips and ideas with people as they stop by her booth. Rachel is always willing to learn-her BA in Creative Writing being just a small part of her education. During the winter months, Rachel has been participating in an online farmers market which allows for buyers to browse and read about Rachel and her products, order, and then pick up the items ordered on Saturday mornings. It is not the same as an in-person market, but Rachel enjoys it just the same.

Rachel updates her blog (SecondTimeAroundHomestead.com[1]) with anecdotal homesteading updates. Some of these are seasonal updates and some are educational, for those wanting to begin a similar lifestyle. She also writes and publishes a variety of book reviews to the blog. She just published an eCourse for crocheting one of her more popular hat designs, and soon there will be an eCourse very similar to this series.

Rachel enjoys a variety of activities in her limited spare time from hiking and kayaking in warmer months, to reading and crocheting in colder months. Rachel enjoys baking, both sweet and savory treats, for her family. She also has a variety of episodic stories publishing and a children's book that was recently released. Other family members enjoy hunting and fishing while she prefers foraging. They all love the water, though many of them prefer warm summer water versus "hard" (frozen) water. They all have hiked and snowshoed extensively.

You can also find us on various social media such as Facebook, Instagram, Pinterest, TikTok,...

---

1. http://www.secondtimearoundhomestead.com

How to begin homesteading with hardly any space and you work full time...

Some of my favorite books as a kid were the ones with young adults who became self-sustaining. It was a no-brainer that I hoped to do the same. I had grown up with a garden, but by no means was that enough to feed myself or my family in a self-sustaining way! We have succeeded at this point to have me quit my off-homestead job and for my husband to cut back on his hours.* Within a couple years, we should be completely self-employed. Take what we learned and make it yours in your self-sufficiency/homesteading dream.

* Note: While we are still capable of this, since the first printing I have gone back to work to speed our journey to retirement. Our plans ever change. This keeps us on the partially self-sufficient, instead of the mostly self-sufficient path.

What is homesteading?

ASK TEN PEOPLE AND you will probably get ten different answers as to what "homesteading" actually means. You need to decide your own working definition and that is the only one that will matter. You may want to be able to benefit by working the land and harvesting from it. Or, you may want your own fresh eggs or meat and know how the animals were treated. You may want to have a huge store set up of preserves and canned goods. Or, you may want to live completely off the grid and work only for yourself.

Realistically, there are "urban homesteaders" living in apartments and supplementing their existence with a potted plant garden and preserving foods from the local farmers market. There are people living in the Wilds of Alaska who only come to town once or twice a year. It really is up to you.

We live about ten minutes from the nearest grocery store. We own about four acres, but we are lucky enough to have fantastic neighbors who let us forage and hunt on their lands, as well as good friends with whom we work to sugar or sometimes have large crops. I buy raw milk from a friend and we often buy local produce beyond what we grow. This is what works for us.

Since the beginning

FOR AS LONG AS I CAN remember, I have been cooking and baking almost from scratch (some scratch and some bought canned goods) as well as gardening. Soft, homemade chocolate chip cookies are the best!

For many holidays, I would create my gifts from hobbies such as baking, sewing, or crocheting. Teacher gifts were often a jar of jam and a craft the kids and I did together.

I remember first learning to sew a button back on when I was still young, and when my children were young I patched a lot of holes and tears and they learned the simple stitches. My husband, a welder, was constantly burning his shirts. At one point we jokingly said that some of his shirts were more patches than the original shirt. I've never been very good at replacing zippers, but I haven't practiced either. We continue to gain skills every year from childhood through retirement.

Dreams

When I was a little girl, I wanted a mansion. Something like my Barbie® dolls had, with gorgeous rooms, cool furniture, and a pool... Then, I decided that a cottage on a mountain away from people would be great, just a dog and cat for company. Then, I realized that I needed other animals for milk, eggs, and meat, plus maybe wool or pelts.

Now is the time that you need to really consider *your* dreams. Solidify these concepts into an actual plan. It can still be a loose plan and you can always adjust the plan, but no matter how spontaneous you want to be, you need a plan. Dreams are fantastic, but most are achieved through planning.

The First Year

PLANNING IS WHAT YOU really need to do this first year, but you probably want to dive right in, too. The absolute most important thing here is to find your direction and not overextend yourself. It is really easy to dabble (or dive right in) to all sorts of little things and then find yourself falling behind. One day you wake up exhausted, frustrated, and maybe beyond recovery for that year. It happens. It's ok, not ideal, but ok. Refocus on you, your family, and any animals that you need to care for. The creatures and people you care for are non-negotiable, anything else can wait.

First, prioritize what you want to achieve in the long run. Second, value/evaluate what you have right now. Third, come up with the next steps both immediate and in the next couple of years. Fourth, hope that there isn't some world-altering event like a pandemic to completely affect your plans.

Be ready, something always will come up whether it is a pandemic, or late frost, illness, or a gas shortage (which affects so many other things), etc. If all our plans were based solely upon our own abilities, we probably wouldn't fall behind. Unfortunately, other things do affect us and unforeseen (or hoped against) events do happen. You must leave a buffer in your planning to account for these.

Always, always, always re-evaluate and be willing to adjust as you learn what to repeat or expand. Start small, succeed, expand.

Choosing your Location

IF YOU ALREADY HAVE the land that you want - fantastic!! Your next planning will be how to most effectively use your land in the short term and as you expand. If you already have infrastructure (barns, garden, lumber, etc.), you may want to skim some parts of this book. You still need an amendable plan.

If not, some of your initial planning needs to be on how to achieve the property you want. Can you actively pursue land now or do you need to build up savings and credit? When choosing your land, you want to consider if you want to be near family, what climate you want, are you more interested in gardening, animals, foraging,...and what properties are best for the activities you want to do. Just as important, is to consider what views make you the happiest. Are you most happy when you see mountains? A body of water? Fields waving for miles? Choose what makes you happy to see at random moments throughout your day.

Career

IN YOUR IDEAL WORLD, will you continue the career you have now (or a different one) while homesteading or do you hope to have your homestead self-sufficient enough that you do not need an outside source of income? You should also consider other benefits offered by jobs such as health insurance and retirement funds. Even discounts offered by particular jobs may make working part-time completely worth it to your little homestead. Many homesteaders work at feed or clothing stores in part for the discount offered. Others choose to work as a bartender so they can work once a week and as they feel like it for extra money, this gives them flexibility around the busy seasons.

Our family has continued working outside of our homestead, while starting slowly. This means we had steady paychecks coming in, but on the flip side there was not nearly as much time to garden, hunt, or preserve. Some years we were still stacking firewood in the snow (I do not recommend this!).

Within three years, we hope to have both of us home full time and not only holding steady but also building up a retirement. There were a number of ways we could have done this, a number of different ways and perhaps have arrived to this point sooner, but then we might not have had some of the family activities that we did. Life is a constant series of choices and reevaluation.

Partially self-sufficient

PARTIALLY SELF-SUFFICIENT really covers a huge gambit from the hobbyist, to the people who harvest and produce much of what they use on a daily basis.This is where we fall. I do not choose this life for religious purposes or for a large fear of our supply chain. That being said, I appreciate the fact that if the food supply chain in the US fails, my family will not starve, we will not have the comforts that we are used to, but we will not starve or flounder. We also appreciate that when we raise the animals or grow our foods, we have a much better understanding of how they were raised/grown and literally, what went into them.

In our partial self-sufficiency we have a garden, but we also buy produce. We forage and hunt. We preserve some foods and buy plenty of others. We do not mill any of our own grains or coffees. We enjoy take-out. We have backyard chickens for the eggs and meat. We also buy chicken breasts or chicken thighs at the store. We often buy our firewood log length, and cut & split it ourselves. We mend some of our clothes, and I crochet plenty of winter hats, but we purchase the majority of our clothes and all of our footwear. We may use salves and tinctures, but we buy plenty of OTC medicines, too. We have the supplies, skills, and tools to reload our own ammunition, but often choose to buy it a box at a time. The same for fishing, we have everything we need, or the ability to find it, but often we value our time more and buy a dish of worms for $3 or the bucket of baitfish for $12.

Mostly self-sufficient

THIS IS A LEVEL THAT many people strive for. Many people have huge gardens and forage all year for fresh produce. Of this, what isn't eaten fresh is then frozen, dried, canned, or somehow preserved for later use in the year. These people may still purchase what cannot be grown in their area, say bananas in Vermont for example, or buy surplus amounts for what they want to preserve. More than likely, they grow and dry their own herbs for flavoring food, teas, tinctures, salves, soaps, etc. These people will decide how much meat they want to raise each year and raise an appropriate amount of birds and animals. They may supplement with fishing and hunting.

Many of these people raise bees or tap sugar trees for their sweeteners for the year. Many of these people harvest their own fuel for the homestead whether it is wind, wood, biodiesel, solar...More than likely they have their own water source.

While we easily assume what these mostly self-sufficient people do for their homestead (ie. gardening, livestock, etc) we may forget about what they do for medical needs, clothes, furniture, etc. If you hope to be mostly self-sufficient, then you must also have or learn the skills to repair your machines and furniture, to weave or knit or sew together fabrics and pelts for your clothes for all the daily and weather needs. It is often medical needs that move the "mostly self-sufficient" to "partially self-sufficient." Some medical technologies just cannot be grown, built, or maintained on most homesteads.

Entirely self-sufficient

THIS IS PRETTY EXTREME and not the life that most people will choose. I personally like the convenience of going to the grocery store for my bags of flour, my canisters of coffee, even my milk, so I can skip caring for a dairy cow. Though, there is nothing quite like raw milk, I do love it! I choose to buy raw milk instead of the cow.

This will be a multistep process, do not expect to achieve being entirely self-sufficient in one year. I would also recommend trying to build up a store of non-perishable foods in case you have some sort of tragedy, crop failure, illness (yourself or animals). There are many things and events that can interfere with our dreams. As with any project, you can mitigate the effects by planning ahead.

Prioritizing Your Focus

MORE THAN LIKELY, YOU will overlap on some of the aspects of homesteading and self-sufficiency that interest you. You still need to focus on the priorities so that you don't become completely overwhelmed by spreading your focus and your time too thin. Certainly, it may make sense that you want a large garden if you also hope to can or preserve a great deal. However, please remember, many things all come ready to harvest at the same time, and you need to allow time for the harvesting and the prepping and the canning and the clean-up if you want to do both fresh and preserved. It's better to start small and be successful than to bite off more than you can chew and fail at most of it. Maybe you have a garden to eat fresh food from while canning only five things, and you raise a half dozen chickens simultaneously. Absolutely, you can achieve this! Are you going to focus most of the rest of your time on hunting and fishing to add to your diet? Maybe you care less about growing and foraging your own food, but you really want to create your own product (soap, wool, raw milk, hemp,...) on your homestead. Any choice is valid, but you need to decide where to focus. Start small, succeed, and expand!

Some Things To Consider In Depth, Before Buying Property

Water Sources

We all know that water is key to survival. However, have you actually thought about what you *need* water for and what you *want* water for? Many of us are used to turning a knob and having as much water as we need. When you are looking to purchase land, or where to build on your property, you need to look deeper at this.

Know your water sources on your land. Do you have a spring? A well? A pond? A river? How much effort do you need to put into this source to make it easily usable? How much supply is there? A full pond in the spring may be almost dry by mid summer. What water rights do you have? Just because you have a river doesn't mean that you have access to all that water. Is the water potable? Is it considered safe for gardening and animals but not for humans? Is this likely to change? Are there easements for you to access water offsite or for others to access water on your property?

Just as important as knowing what water you have access to, is knowing what you want to have water for. You probably use far more water than you realize to drink and cook with, also to clean yourself and your home. Now consider whether you need water for animals and gardens or orchards. Weather, of course, plays a part in this equation too, as hot dry weather will raise your watering needs for any living thing you take care of.

Can you legally collect rainwater in this location? Is it practical to collect and use rainwater? What about gray water? (This is water that has been used but not sewage water. For example, some people save their water from washing dishes to water their garden.)

Where do you want water accessibility? At my house it is easy to run a hose from our outside house faucet to the garden and to the chicken pen. But if I had a barn full of cows, I would not want to be filling individual water containers by hose and carrying them. Consider how climate affects this. My easy hose reach is not applicable in winter as outdoor lines freeze. Late fall through early spring I fill waterers inside my bathtub and carry them out to the chickens at least twice a day, sometimes more often. With a flock of less than thirty, this is manageable; with a herd of large mammals, it would not be realistic.

Easements and Right of Ways

EASEMENTS AND RIGHT of ways are not just about water sources. These need to be considered in terms of accessing properties and resources. Before purchasing any property you must know whether you must grant or if you need access to water, sewer, electric, any utilities, landlocked property, sports trails, etc. Just because it seems obvious that you need access to a resource doesn't make it automatic. Likewise, you may learn that there is a grandfather clause allowing the neighboring property owner to cut through your prime field for access to their back property, or some such. You may also learn that, while not legally approved, your property contains the main trail to a local swimming hole or some such.

Check with the property records at the town or county clerk. But also ask around and see what the locals know. Candid, respectful, conversations may garner interesting information about your property lines as well. Before buying any property, make sure you know your exact lines. You don't want to make a mistake and affect another's property, nor do you want to be taken advantage of.

Road Care & Emergency Access/First Aid

JUST AS IMPORTANT AS knowing the easements and right of ways is knowing who takes care of your road. Most of us assume we are responsible for our own driveway, but what about the road leading up to it. Depending on the class of highway, you may find that neither the town nor the state are required to plow it, grade it, or generally take care of it. On the flip side, if it is property of the town and under their care, you may have to worry about what they do to care for the road. More than likely they will occasionally dig out the ditches and lay down more gravel or repave it. These maintenance tasks will not affect you very much. However, they may also use pesticides and chloride on the roads and you may not want that run-off onto your property. They may even be allowed to widen the road, thereby using more of your property. These are details worth looking into.

Hand in hand with the road care is emergency services. You need to know whether emergency vehicles can travel your road. If you have a very narrow road or a light bridge it may be that the heavy emergency vehicles can't even get to your house. Or maybe they can get to your house, but there is no way to reach an injured person in the back of your property unless they hike in. If you live in a rural area, the emergency service providers will be able to answer these questions. Once you have determined that in ideal weather they can (or can't) reach you, you must take precautions for extreme weather. Will your road flood out? Who clears and sands it during winter storms? Always try to prepare for the worst case scenarios.

Depending on how quickly emergency services can get to you, you may want to create an extensive first aid kit and learn more than basic life saving measures. In the case that someone in your family is bitten by a venomous snake, be sure to call the ER as you travel, in case they need to have the anti-venom flown in. They may not take your word for it, but if they do, every minute can be precious. If you have a life threatening allergy, make sure you have enough epi-pens to get you to the hospital, many people require multiple doses every half hour or so. Ask your doctor! Always have a three day to seven day (or more!) supply of other required medications whether insulin, cardiac, or whatever. You do not want to be stuck home due to a storm and run out of needed medications. Plan for the worst case scenarios; hopefully they never happen.

Emergency Vet

ALONG WITH YOUR OWN health, you need to consider the health of your livestock and pets. Normal care shouldn't be an issue as you can schedule a farm vet out or bring your animals to a veterinarian clinic for their regular care. What about emergencies? What about tough births? You need to know what local, or not so local, resources there are and if any vet will make emergency calls if you live on a class 4 or private road.

Children/Elder Care

TAKING CARE OF CHILDREN or our elders is even more complicated than caring for ourselves. Often, they may need more emergency care as they may not share their initial symptoms with us to warrant an earlier medical visit. They may also need more specialized care. You also need to consider their social health. These members of your family may need more outings and be less happy working long hard days on the homestead. Or, they may be content to spend all day, every day on the homestead but need frequent care or observation which is difficult to do while you are working your homestead. Have a plan to monitor their whole health *throughout* the year and adapt as necessary.

Support Community

FIND YOUR SUPPORT COMMUNITY and it is not all about medical care. Are there mentors for you? What services are offered that you can take advantage of? Talk to some locals, find out what networks there are. You don't want the majority of your support network to be Facebook experts thousands of miles away. Social media is good for many things, but you need some on-the-ground, local support as well. Find out if there are auctions near you, Amish stores, farmers markets, etc. Talk to some old-timers if you can. Tell them straight up what your dream is and ask them their opinion. You may not like all their advice, but they know the local area, culture, and climate. Ask these old-timers about the politics, too. They will be able to tell you whether the government seems to be supportive of homesteaders like you or against you with ridiculous regulations. Buy them a coffee and ***listen***.

Insurances

YOU NEED INSURANCE. As you are considering what you will do and where you will do it, you need to find insurance coverage that matches. For example, many home insurances will not cover a barn or animals. Many insurances will not allow for a woodstove. Does your health insurance consider homesteading to be a high risk occupation? So many questions.

In general, bundling is good but in all reality you need to speak with an agent. Find a local agent and tell them what you want to do and ask their advice. They want to find you the best packages. They want your business, and they understand that it must be affordable and pleasing. They will work with you to find the best coverage for you as that helps them as well.

Proximity and Layout

FIRST AND FOREMOST, you want to consider your proximity to town, to neighbors, and to water sources. Also as mentioned above, you need to consider the access to your property for yourself and others.

Second, how are you going to plan the layout of your property? Take your time with this. If possible, find evidence for how the seasons look on your property. Where does the wind blow the hardest? Where is the most sheltered area? Where is the full sun through the day, and partial sun? You are using this information to consider your house temperature, snow drifts, plant growth, etc.

You need time to consider the layout of the gardens, orchards, pastures, etc. for how they will grow the best in terms of light, water, and weather. Pastures and orchards do not need to be too close to your house, but you probably want the gardens pretty close.

Consider your outbuildings and your animals. For example, our chicken coop is on the far side of the backyard. I wanted it far enough away to not have to smell chicken manure, and to have that manure near the garden. But I don't want the coop too far away when carrying feed or eggs, and especially in the winter when I refresh their water several times a day due to ice. I also wanted a full backyard for play. It is all about balance.

You need to consider how close to the house or barn you want buildings, gardens, and pastures. For example, you may find that the ideal place for your chicken run is near the garden, but you also want to have bee hives near the garden. You only have so much room...is there any reason not to have the bee hives in with the chickens? Turns out that bees and chickens can co-exist pretty easily. However, you want to check where the flight plans are (the most common routes the bees will take to and from food and water sources) so that you aren't frequently walking in their way and getting stung.

Building Knowledge/Repair Knowledge

JUST AS IMPORTANT AS the skills of animal care, gardening, preserving, etc., are the skills of building and repair. Anyone who owns any large equipment should understand their basic care and common fixes. The more you know, the more you can repair independently, the more money you can save by not having to hire someone. Also, you may have less downtime as you won't need to transport the machinery for repair nor wait for someone else's schedule.

Building skills are the same as repair skills. You will end up building far more than you ever imagined from animal and storage structures to fencing, garden beds to clotheslines, to who-knows-what. Basic building skills are necessary, but easy enough to learn. However, these skills are like everything else: start small, succeed, expand. You may find some hidden challenges in an "easy" project, just as you may find that the perfect design you created doesn't work as well as this new one you just found somewhere else.

Have you checked the town and county ordinances? State ordinances too? Federal laws?

CHECK BEFORE YOU START, if you plan on selling any of the foods or products that you will be producing. Many things are allowed for personal consumption that cannot be sold to the public. There are also sometimes rules about how many chickens you can own or how many (if any) roosters. There are other ordinances about types of animals that can be owned. For example goats may be ok, but not guinea hens; peacocks may be allowed but not sheep,...

There are ordinances on selling baked goods, which may control certifying your kitchen, the amount of sales, the packaging. Similar rules may exist for pickles and preserves. Who knew that dog treats would have more regulations than selling human treats?!? I was shocked when my research showed that in our state regulations. Butchered meat is a whole other set of rules and regulations. Often, farmers get around these ordinances by selling the live animal and delivering it to a certified meat processor/butcher, whom the buyer picks up from. Do your own research.

Even simple things like the "free" by-products, as in selling manure or feathers, have a whole set of regulations.

Look into what you can or can't own. Look into what the regulations are for caring for your animals (you don't want to receive animal abuse charges because you provided a three sided structure with a movable wall instead of a permanent, four-sided structure...). Look into what you need for selling in terms of taxes, licenses, scales, facilities, labeling, quantity, and other details.

How do you Reward Yourself?

IF YOU ARE USED TO rewarding yourself with multiple vacations (or even one) a year, you probably don't want to be self-sustaining with farm animals. We have had only barnyard fowl and household pets for years. Yet this was enough to prevent us from spontaneous weekends away and certainly not weeklong vacations. As we expand our ventures over the next two years, it will be impossible.

Some rewards are to buy the equipment to make our tasks easier. For example, the laptop I type this on is a huge upgrade from my prior cheap laptop. This was a reward to myself *and* makes my life easier. Likewise, I bought myself a heavy duty sewing machine last year. I was able to sew almost everything I wanted on my regular machine, but now I can sew through thicker materials more easily and with far fewer broken needles. It may be for work that I bought the machine, but because it is so much more efficient, I can accomplish more in less time, allowing me more "free" time each day. Maybe I don't take advantage of that free time to relax, but it does lessen the stress I was carrying.

This isn't to say that you can't do anything fun for you personally. There are plenty of day trips or meals out that you can do. Working for yourself, means that once the animals are taken care of, you can take an afternoon off to go fishing, or kayaking, or skiing, or sit in the hammock with margaritas. Maybe you can even barter with someone and arrange care for your animals for a day and you can sneak away for a weekend - it just gets more complicated.

Three lessons in the first six months that we said we really were homesteaders

From our blog[1], originally posted 8/29/2020

Plans Change – plans change a lot!

THE FIRST LESSON IS one I have known for a long time, but it is so important we're going to treat it like a new lesson: No matter what you have planned, something is going to change. Every single time you have a day planned out so you can accomplish tons, something is going to come up that takes immediate precedence and you will work on that for the majority of your time and energy and only accomplish a bare minimum of your other plan.

For example, today, I had a full day of school work, cleaning, baking, dehydrating, gardening, and sewing planned. Instead, I cooked and cleaned only the minimum of cooking and cleaning, and instead focused on resumes and job applications for my son and husband as their intention for the summer changed. Also, energy was put into changing out, cleaning up, and reorganizing barnyard fowl for the about to arrive ducklings. And then, suddenly I had to

1. https://secondtimearoundhomestead.com/2020/08/29/three-things-i-have-learned-in-the-first-six-months-of-really-homesteading/

transport them, too. There was no real cleaning, no blankets washed, no baking, no dehydrating, and no sewing. Not even reading happened and I sometimes get paid for that.

We don't even need to talk about Covid-19 – that changed all the plans.

Gardens do not care about your plans

The second lesson is the garden will not do as you plan. I bought a greenhouse this year and started a bunch of seedlings in the basement. I hoped to grow a bunch of herbs and get a jumpstart on the veggies. The greenhouse was easy to put up and stayed warm and moist, which was fantastic. Until, we stopped heating the basement because it was warm enough to not need the wood stove. The light in the greenhouse was not warm enough on its own. Eventually the seedlings got mildew-y and sickly. Very few of them successfully transplanted. I shall try again next spring, but with more wood to keep a steady temp in the basement until I can plant outdoors. Meanwhile, the weather has been a bit uncooperative, but it always is. I ended up being given some tomato starts and those are fantastic. We bought some cucumber and squash starts and those are great too. The directly sewn cucumber, peas, beans, lettuces, spinach, carrots, and beats are slow, but good. The sunflowers are hit or miss, but I'm pretty sure I was battling chipmunks and some stray chickens in the beginning which ravaged my seeds. This was the first year planting morning glories and they seem to be doing well.

Meet Red. She's quite good at escaping their pen, but she also goes back in every night to sleep in the coop.

SO, I HAD HOPED TO have lots of veggies for eating fresh and freezing. We'll have the fresh, but I'm not sure about preserving it.

I hoped to have herbs to use fresh, to dry, and to attempt making teas with. Only the parsley seems to be doing well, most dies in the greenhouse.

Sunflowers are for us to eat and for the chickens. Also I had hoped to have a wall of them by the driveway. I think the small creatures stole most of the seeds by the driveway. We'll see how the seed harvest goes.

Morning glories were for prettiness by the stone wall, which looks promising, and for an attempt at resined jewelry. We'll see. The plants seem to be doing well, but it's too early for blooms yet. Meanwhile I've been practicing on pansies, and soon we'll try daylilies.

Money is fickle

The third is that if you have any savings, there will be an unexpected expense whether it is the car, the washing machine, the fridge...

Selling a product from your homestead is a great idea. Consider your realistic timeframes and don't overextend yourself.

I sell these fantastic, reusable market totes[2], made from empty feedbags (I had a bunch of empty chicken ones and hated throwing them away...). I decided to reach out to several local stores all in the same evening to see if they would carry our bags. I have spent the last week sewing A LOT of bags.

---

2. https://goimagine.com/clothing/bags-and-purses/upcycled-blue-and-white-wrangler-ranch-market-tote-clone/?action=preview&s_storefront=1

In progress, market totes...

See above for my hopes to begin making our own teas – that will be next year instead. Likewise I had hoped to make some sage bundles, and body products, but that will be pushed off a year too, unless I decide to buy some herbs at farm stands. Instead, we'll focus on sewn products and flower jewelry. My daughter found a dead butterfly too, that we'll try making into a piece of jewelry. I would never kill one for this purpose, but to resin it and enjoy it long term after its natural death, seems just fine. I'm always open to new ideas and I save tons of photographs/screenshots. It is completely easy to be scattered and lose focus and never finish any projects. While there are so many crafts I would like to do, I have spent the summer focusing on tote sales and learning to resin.

Lastly, we all know that the work is never done, but it's never done.

As summer winds down and I'm going back to working in school full time I have had to prioritize what canning and preserving needs to be done vs what I want to do. Likewise, the freezer breaking down with none available for less than the price of a cheap car, I have had to reconsider my food preservation and foraging. I need to prepare the chicken coop for winter, decide whether there is time to plant flower bulbs to cheer me in the summer, and clean up the yards for winter. Moving firewood to stacks near the stove really needs to be a priority... Sometimes I just need to breathe, too.

So how does this help us prepare for the next six months? Well the prep now, like firewood, has obvious benefits to the next 6 months, most of which are freezing cold. But also, it helps us to plan for the six months following the next six months. Where do I expect to be, projectwise at this time next year? What was too ambitious? What was easy? What can we prepare for better? None of us expected a worldwide pandemic, but let's have two sets of plans for next Spring – still shut down, and not shut down. Because we have absolutely no idea.

Accountability and Evaluation

EVERY STEP OF THE WAY you need to evaluate what you have done, what you wanted to do, and what you need to to adjust. Sometimes, your plans work better than you expected, often, you end up finding something successful and you can ride that wave in a manner you didn't expect, and sometimes the best laid plans fail. The key things you need to see are *what your actions need to be going forward* to harness the successes and fix or avoid the failures. Remember, start small, succeed, expand.

Right now is a great time to find yourself a notebook or binder to start collecting your information, recording your dreams and plans, and to record your questions and observations. I have files on the computer, but also notebooks.

I don't keep records on our chickens because we have less than 30. I have a good idea of how many eggs we should be getting daily through the year, and I see the girls each day as I let them out of the coop each morning. They chatter to me when I close up the coop every night, but often I don't close it until after dark and it is difficult to see individual birds. If I had a field of cattle or animals needing vaccinations, or needing to monitor breeding, I would certainly need better records.

I do have records for where I sell my bags, where I have received empty feedbags from, etc. As we expand what we sell, I'll expand these records. I have records of the garden, what I planted when and the yield. My garden records are always better in the spring and early summer than in the late summer and fall as harvest takes precedence over record keeping. I have records of my writing assignments and I have several apps that help me monitor our social media and blog. Likewise, our selling online through several platforms have built in inventory, sales, etc. Before you start, you want to consider your taxes and what records and receipts you need to complete these.

I sometimes include our accountability right on our blog. Hopefully others can also learn from our success and failures. The following was first posted on 10/31/20 on our blog[3].

---

3. https://secondtimearoundhomestead.com/2020/10/31/autumn-accountability-our-first-year/

Autumn Accountability - The First Year

We're quickly rushing out of October into November. The calendar may say we're in the middle of fall, but realistically (as the snow falls every few days) we're at the end of autumn. Time for our seasonal accountability. Autumn is filled with a lot of tasks that happen every year for us regardless of whether we say we are homesteaders or not.

Firewood

As I write this in the end of October, we have 2 cords of firewood in the basement. We have a little more than a cord that we cut and split ready to be moved into the basement. And, we have two cords being delivered today (to move to the basement). The youngest, my almost 13 year old, has been throwing the wood into the basement through our bulkhead. Then, I toss it to the other end of the basement, where the woodstove is, and finally, I stack it. Honestly, I have only a little over a cord stacked so far... I always want 6+ cords ready to burn. I hate rationing wood and being cold. We heat solely with the woodstove, so we need enough for September through April or more.

Garden

I harvested lots of green tomatoes and froze some for green tomato cake, after the first hard frost. Potatoes were dug soon after. The puppy knocked over the sunflowers so the heads were brought in to finish drying. The herbs were picked and hung to dry. Except, because the parsley was so healthy, even after frost, I transplanted one of the plants to a pot and we're continuing to grow it inside. We'll see if it works. Right now it doesn't seem as vibrant, but it's not getting that direct sunlight either. Usually, we transplant to the outdoors, not to the inside!

The last lawn mow of the season included a lot of fallen leaves. These were collected and dumped into the garden as a compost mulch. We don't put any chemicals on our grass, so this is safe for our food supply, aka the garden.

There is still horseradish to harvest, wash, and grind. I just haven't gotten to it yet.

After harvesting the horseradish, I need to clean out the last tomato cages and such. Then spread the leaves/grass clippings, and some aged woodshavings & poop from the chicken coop.

Fowl

Last year was the first year we raised turkeys and they were behemoths. This year we butchered them in the beginning of October so that they were all in 15-30# range. The challenge with butchering 6 turkeys is having enough freezer space.

The chickens and ducks don't mind the colder weather, but we are getting fewer eggs, most likely because of the shorter days. We don't usually use a heat lamp in the coop until the eggs start freezing, but we may start earlier this year to extend the days. Right now, at the end of October, it is only light from about 7am until 6:30pm

School & work routines

Due to Covid-19 the kids' school year started later per an order from the governor. I started right on time, though as staff began "early" to prepare for the new Covid restrictions. It has been a crazy year so far, with social distancing, wearing masks, each child in a different form of learning (online, hybrid, in-person)... Sports practices are different too. Because there were so many restrictions, the youngest chose not to play football. The younger girl played soccer with a mask, and I coached elementary X-Country running (nomasks while running). Unfortunately, many games were canceled for the year as schools limited contact and eventually the state dictated no interstate travel.The XCountry meets were not held in conjunction with the high school races, so we scheduled three within our district (7 schools, four teams). Unfortunately, two schools went virtual for a week (our son's was one) canceling one race.

But the routine of packing my lunch, some school lunches, and sometimes a lunch for hubby, was pretty solid. By October, I finally had some time on the weekends to make items for the lunches like granola, cookies, jello cups. We can still improve over the single serving granola bars, beef jerky etc, but we have kept the routine of buying large packages of crackers, chips, etc and divvying into smaller containers or bags.

Preserving

So with so many people home for Coronacation, there were many more gardeners. As soon as the seed shortage became known I started buying some jars here and there. But there hasn't been that many available and I refused to buy them at $30/case...So we didn't can as much as normal. Then, the freezer broke so I had less room to freeze.

We did make two batches of dilly beans, the youngest helped with one. I intended to do salsa and pasta sauce, maybe bread and butter pickles. I didn't even make applesauce.

I did try out some new things. Using the dehydrator, I made some veggie powder. I started with beet because I can hide something sweet in a lot of things. It is super pretty! Then we also tried some flavored finishing salts.I made some merlot salt. I always forget to try it with my steak. I've sprinkled it on a few things and it's pretty good. I want to try it with some other flavors. Maybe this is a future holiday gift idea.

Homestead Sales

This is a focus I've been working on. During the first part of Coronacation I became active on our blog. Part two has been expanding our sales. I began making bags like crazy and finding places to sell them at. I had actually started this before the world shut down, but that gave me time to actually work on it. Then craft fairs didn't happen, or farmers markets, but I began setting up our blog to be an actual website with sales. This fall, I have done one in-person craft fair and several online fairs.

My new focus is on creating subscription packages. I have some great ideas, but marketing is not my strength. Look for it soon, we'll have a subscription package for our bags, for our homestead items, and maybe Vermont Tourism.

We weren't able to have garden products for sale, but I did start making jewelry. I have wanted to make upcycled jewelry from bottle caps and can tabs. I'm learning as I go, but I think they are pretty cool so far. I need some beads and chains, but I have plenty of bottle caps. *giggle*

Looking ahead to winter

I always hope that the next season will be slower, but it never seems to happen. I do hope to read more and craft more. Most of all, I hope to write more.

Soon the wood will be inside and stacked. Soon the horseradish will be ground and frozen. Then I should have time to read, write, and craft.

Winter weather also tends to lead to more soups and casseroles. There is nothing quite as nice as coming home to the smells of dinner almost ready. I use both the crock pot and the oven settings to have dinner almost ready when we're scheduled to be home. We have no idea what the winter sports schedule will be, we assume ski racing is still on, but we'll be ready.

Looking ahead to the Holidays

With Covid-19 still running rampant, a few days before Halloween everything was still a huge question. Our cousin, Gary, loves Halloween and was looking forward to 2020 for years: full moon, Saturday, time change (longer night). Even the weather was fairly cooperative looking. Masks fit right in, but Covid-19 fears are not the same as fun-scary fears.

Thanksgiving is a big deal for many families, and again Covid-19 seems to be overshadowing the holiday. As we finish October, we're awaiting word from the state as to whether all schools will be required to be remote learning following Thanksgiving to accommodate families and quarantining. It's out of our hands, of course, but will have a large impact on our lives.

So, moving onto Christmas. We don't know how much family and friends we may see, but we know that we shall celebrate it at home. This is true for our friends of other cultures and faiths, as well, we all seem to at least be planning a home celebration of some sort.

I started purchasing some items as they are on sale (passes for the local mountain, for example), but some of the factory sales are just not happening this year. Sadness. Every couple years, she goes to the factory sale for Darn Tough

Socks, spends about a hundred dollars and walks out with hundreds of dollars of product. We hoped to do the same with TurtleFur this year.

We clearly never know what is going to happen, but we can reflect on our accomplishments and missed deadlines. We can keep on trying.

What are your big goals for five years from now? Ten years? Retirement?

You need to consider your big goals and long term goals as these are what guide your decisions now. Here is where you consider if you want to remain a Hobby Homestead or you want to be continuously growing and becoming more self-sufficient. More than likely, you create your own level of challenge and comfort. This brings us back to the questions a few pages back about whether you wanted to supplement your shopping with homestead products or you want to become mostly self-sufficient and supplement your homestead. It is just as important to remember that plans are always changing and goals can be different at different points in our lives.

As you consider your long term plans you must consider three things in the forefront: your savings/income, your health, your desires to travel or to relax. Compare what you find when you examine these three concepts to how you homestead. Is what you are doing now, what you want in 15 years? Will you be able to physically do the work then, that you are required to do now? Or maybe you work your buns off now and as you need to, you scale back and work less as the years go by.

Honestly, this is what keeps us at a Hobby Level Homestead. I'm not purchasing hundreds of acres and buying hundreds of heads of animals when we want to be scaling back in a few years. Instead, I'm focussing our "expanding" energies towards sustainable activities for us, such as my freelance writing.

You really need to look deep for your choices, and you need to be willing to update your plans as you go. It goes back to prioritizing your focus and constantly re-evaluating. Start small. Succeed. Expand.

Just the fact that you are reading through this book and doing some soul searching and research tells me that you are off to a great start on this journey to begin your Homestead. Chase your dreams, but do your research, too!

We would love to hear from you on your journey. Stop by our blog[1], Facebook[2], or Instagram[3], and let us know how you are doing!

---

1. http://www.secondtimearoundhomestead.com
2. https://www.facebook.com/SecondTimeAroundHomestead/
3. https://instagram.com/secondtimearoundhomestead

How To Make Money From Your Hobby Homestead

Enjoy your homestead *AND* earn an income

Message from Rachel

This book is written to be like a self-directed, self-paced eCourse. You may choose to skip episodes that don't relate to your interests. Likewise, you may jump around through them following your interests. There are many ways that this book could be laid out and the order in which to cover each subject. Ultimately, I wrote this in the order that made sense to me. (Although I changed the order many times!) However, you can go through it in any order you choose. I encourage you **not** to try everything at once! Start small, succeed, then expand. Take risks when you can, but ALWAYS have a back up plan!

I strongly recommend that you begin with the first lecture "So You Want to Make Money?" and review different types of income (and savings) as well as set your own expectations and goals. I would very much like you to finish with the end survey so that I can have feedback on what worked the best for you and what ideas you have for improvement.

Take your time with this and find what works best for you! Make your plans, but always be willing to adapt.

Chapter 1 - So you want to make money here, huh?

Setting your goals - What are your expectations?

Consider these questions, and we would love to see your answers email us:

With the money you have right now (imagine you had no more income), how many days will you survive (food, medications, utilities, gasoline/fares, etc.)?

How much income do you need to have in order to live at the standard you want?

Are you essentially living paycheck to paycheck or do your assets (what puts money into your pocket) exceed your liabilities (what takes money out of your pocket)? How great is this divide?

How many streams of income do you have? Do you have passive income?

Are you happy with the balance between your time and your income?

What are your financial goals for the next five years? Ten years? Rest of your life?

How can you improve your economics this month?

You really need some goals and reasonable expectations. Maybe you're a millionaire and you can buy everything you want, try it out, and settle on what you like best. Most likely this isn't the case though. A little planning in the beginning can go a long way.

My motto is "Start small. Succeed. Expand." Have a large goal. Then break it into pieces. Make those successful and then keep growing. You cannot possibly succeed by trying to do it all, all at once.

Saving money is making money

It is really satisfying to work hard, earn money, and then put it away for a fun time or a rainy day. However, sometimes it is better to work half as much, save money, and have extra time in the bank to enjoy yourself or relax, rather than busting your butt more.

There is a time and a place for passive income to work for you, and to use your hobbies to make money WHILE you play. But, incorporate at least some of these ways to save money and you'll be even further ahead.

You might be interested in this post on our blog "Five Easy Ways to Save Money[1]" whether you are saving for the holidays or just for a "little extra":

Make your money work for you - passive income

JUST WHAT IS PASSIVE Income?

1. https://secondtimearoundhomestead.com/2020/11/14/money-tight-for-the-holidays-5-easy-ways-to-save-money/

Not very long ago I read a book called *Rich Dad, Poor Dad* by Robert Kiyosaki. I really wish I had read this when I was about 20, but better late (40's) than never. You may know a little about passive income - it's the idea that you can be passive (not actively working) and somehow you earn money. The best understood example would be investing. Most people know that you can take a risk and invest in something, then hopefully the worth of that something increases and miraculously you make money without doing anything else.

This is awesome, but maybe just a little rosy. Who doesn't wish that they could find the next "Google" or "Apple" or "bitcoin" and invest $100 to become a billionaire not too many years later? You could do this. First, you need to educate yourself or make friends with someone who knows this stuff to steer you to a perfect investment. Then, you need a spare $100 to invest. You need to find the right way to invest to buy that $100 worth of shares with few fees and full control. Lastly, you need the guts to do it. It may work. Or, you may lose it all.

You may have to start small, but you can have passive income in other ways, too.

Education, but not necessarily schooling

There is a general concept in our schools that one must do extended study in a school setting to earn large quantities of wealth.

There are too many fallacies in this concept, as it completely ignores the trades, income versus salary, and learning other skills.

One can choose to complete 4-12 years of formal education post high school, or one can choose to complete an apprenticeship or 1-4 years of trade school and have the SAME hourly wage possibilities WITHOUT the huge school loans.

One may also decide to do a "traditional" 4 year college education and then work up the corporate ladder. Slowly climbing the ladder and making sure that one is making a little money for oneself while making profits for the business owner.

One may also choose to find work that pays the daily/monthly bills and continue educating themselves to better their skills. Maybe first improving skills for the better job within the company, but hopefully learning skills to improve the rest of their life. Learning about investing, learning about real estate, learning the economic laws that may help. First and foremost the focus should be on learning skills to make your money work for you.

Apps that pay

You can start small, like downloading an app that will pay you just for having it run on your phone. It collects the same data as your other apps, but when that data is sold you get a piece of the earnings. Join my team[2] on *Tapestri* and you'll see just what I mean. (By following my link you can join for free, and I receive $1 because you joined my team.) This is controversial as many people don't want an app tracking all they do. However, if you use technology you are already being tracked. In fact, many of those user agreements you sign when you download a new app, gives them permission to track you. *Tapestri* helps you get paid for the data that is already being tracked.

You can also use an app like *RobinHood*. You get $5 of free stock invested when you join. You can choose to invest more. Even if you never invest more, it is quite amusing to see how your stock rises and falls and since it was free money to start (no chance of loss) it's never a risk.

Free money, but not quite passive, are apps likeCoinOp[3] andFetch[4]. In these apps you scan receipts for what you have already bought and you earn money or points for each receipt. If that seems like too much work, you can link the accounts to Amazon and your email, and those virtual receipts automatically earn you your points and coins. Eventually, you can cash out for actual cash or an Amazon gift card.

2. https://refer.tapestri.io/c/1706
3. https://coinout.com/referrals/new?r=ADFQWW2
4. https://fetchrewards.onelink.me/vvv3/referralemail?code=FNB7U

(Again, following my links here can earn me extra points at no cost to you.)

Affiliate Codes

If you can find a way to publish affiliate codes you can earn money or free products. Just above this in the "Apps that Pay" is my affiliate link for Tapestri. You can include links almost anywhere. However legally, you often must disclose that you may benefit through the code.

Consider whether blogging is your niche.

Perhaps you're more interested in being a social influencer on TikTok and Instagram.

You may even be such an expert that you wish to write and sell a course. Or, you finish a course and wish to promote it.

Investing

This is one economic area that the "rich" have an advantage over the "poor" or "working classes". Investing requires a little extra money, if you don't have extra it is impossible to risk it in an investment. Any investment can be a fantastic success or a dismal failure. Can you afford to take this risk?

This is an area that most people, especially those without a lot of extra capital (funds available), start slowly. Most people are able to invest a little, hopefully make money from that investment and invest more. As they have more capital available they may be willing to complete riskier investments which can pay out at a higher rate (and lose at a higher rate).

There are entire courses about investment, in fact, entire educational degrees about this topic. I am not going to teach it here. I absolutely believe you should find some resources to educate yourself, and at least initially work with an expert in the field. As you become more competent, you can certainly control more of the research and decisions.

There are many types of investments from real estate to bonds; bitcoin was heavily in the news. You can also invest in another's business and some people choose to invest in collectibles. There is no right or wrong "thing" to invest in. Depending on your age and your willingness for risk you might want a diversified and (relatively) safe mutual fund, or you may want high risk day trading. Start small, succeed, and expand.

My last piece of advice, and I am not a professional, this is my personal opinion, is that it may be lucrative to find a way to invest the same money repeatedly. For example, let's say that I choose to invest $20 in a low level stock. It's not worth much but it seems like it will steadily grow. I can lose that $20 and still survive comfortably. Maybe we give up ice cream, soda, and chips for a week, but my bills are still paid. Eventually, I make that $20 back so that I now have $40 invested. I withdraw my original $20 and reinvest it in something else. I'm still earning money on my first investment and now I have a new investment from that same $20.

Make your money work for you.

Multiple Streams Of Income

ALWAYS HAVE MULTIPLE streams of income, even if some are only a trickle

What does it mean to have multiple streams of income? Exactly what it sounds like, you should have a variety of ways to earn money that may or may not be related.

Homesteading is a perfect setup for multiple streams of income. This is when you must consider what you enjoy and what you want. You also must consider what resources and skills you have or can attain.

For example, let's say that you will have barnyard fowl. I recommend starting with chickens, but it is easy to branch out to ducks, turkeys, quail, etc. The two obvious income streams are meat and eggs. You might choose to do both, but it's likely you will choose one or the other. So eventually you can make back your money spent on the equipment and feed. Maybe eventually even pay off the coop and fencing.

Now let's take those same fowl with the same expenses and same income. How can you find another way to make money off of them? Fertilized eggs? Can you sell their manure? What about their pretty feathers? (There are sometimes restrictions about selling feathers, and definitely when it comes to selling wild bird feathers so check laws and regulations.) Can you do something with your leftover eggshells?

What can you do with these same fowl for minimum more expense? You can sell fertilized eggs for no extra cost. But if you invest in an incubator you can sell day old chicks for more. Invest more and you can raise and sell pullets.

Cutting expenses is just as important as earning money. So look into free sources of food for them (restaurants, cafe's, daycares) whoever has food scraps that they are throwing away. However, you do want to take some precautions. No raw egg, for example or they will get used to eating raw eggs and then they will eat their own. What about shavings for the coop and the nesting boxes? Can you find a local woodworking factory and get cheap sawdust or shavings?

Ok, so the chickens and their products are an income stream that you can diversify, plenty of other animals offer similar possibilities. But what happens if disaster strikes your flock? Disease, predators, or even fire? You just lost all those little streams of income if you just lost your flock. But that's ok, you can recover. You can get new eggs, chicks, pullets and rebuild. Meanwhile your OTHER streams of income will hold you through.

Diversify with an income stream not dependent upon your barns or the flock. How about printables? Depending on your abilities you might draw or use a computer, but create a printable product to sell. Use your chickens as inspiration: coloring pages, dot-to-dots, calendar, check lists, planners,.... You might only sell each bundle for $.99 but you can sell these around the clock, year round. And, maybe most importantly, it costs you almost nothing.

Diversify with something else. What is a hobby that you enjoy and how can you make money off of it? Do this again and again. Some of your income streams may be just tiny trickles, some may be merry little streams, and some may become torrential rivers.

Chapter 2 - Your Property's Resources

What do you have?

Often we buy property based upon its location to other places, family, or resources, but we also consider what is available (or not a risk) on the property before we buy. For example you might love to hunt, so you are looking for good forests, but maybe you want to grow huge crops so you are looking for open spaces. We all have our wants and not-wants (flooding, wild fires, proximity to industry may be your not-wants) and they will be unique to you and your dreams. Budget and availability are also deciding factors.

There are entire books devoted to finding the best properties and I am not a realtor nor a real estate lawyer. I will not give you any hard and fast advice except that you should have a list of what you must have, and a list of what you want to have. Maybe the school district is make or break for you, maybe water access is of the utmost importance. Perhaps you really like the property, but the taxes are a killer; maybe you love the open area, but the soil is clay. Take your time and don't rush if you can help it.

Once you have the property, do seasonal walk abouts. If you bought the property in the winter you may be pleasantly surprised with an amazing patch of fiddleheads (a species of fern that is considered an edible delicacy by many, but with a very short window of opportunity). In late summer you might find the perfect fishing spot in a shady brook. There are most likely hidden gems that you can only find at certain times of the year. Learn your property and discover how you can best make use of what you already have.

How do you sell it?

BEST USES

How you choose to use your resources can vary quite a bit based upon your abilities, your desires, the regulations, and the market.

You may decide that you would prefer to hunt and forage to supplement your grocery shopping rather than putting in the hours of toil in a garden. Or, you may decide that the driftwood along your beach is perfect for your crafts. Or, you may decide that you have hundreds of acres available and you can build a small campground. These are all viable options and can make great use of what you have. My best use is not your best use, and vice versa.

I can not stress this idea enough: start small, succeed, then expand. It is very hard to do well when you are spread too thin. It is easy to start a lot of projects, but hard to continue doing them all well when they all get up to speed. If you slowly add in, you will have systems designed to keep everything on track. You will have already had a chance to troubleshoot the early projects and improve them. There will still be some long and hectic days, but you have a much better chance at long term success.

Caveat

No matter what you choose to do, make sure you check the legal requirements and limitations as well as your insurance policies. These two details often change plans in huge ways. You may find that you can own as many animals as you want, but you may not allow the general public near them. You may find that the PYO orchard ideas you have must be located "x" number of feet from rivers and roadways, which isn't actually where the best growing area is. Do your research before you start your projects.

Chapter 3 - Chickens!

Why would you want little dinosaurs?

Beware the Chicken Math

There are a lot of reasons to consider becoming a Chicken Tender, but beware of "Chicken Math". It's easy to decide to buy 6 more and come home with 13 or more! Some locations even have regulations that you must buy at least 12 at a time.

Chickens will make you laugh with their antics, especially if you can watch them free ranging. Many breeds are funny and soon you learn their personalities just like other pets. However, unlike cats, chickens can actually pay for themselves with their products. It's up to you whether you want to save money by raising your own chickens solely for the purpose of knowing how your own eggs or meat were produced, or if you want to sell from your chickens. (NB: you can most likely buy eggs and meat in the store cheaper than you can raise them.

However, the store bought vs farm raised tastes completely different, also you will know if there was any disease or steroids or such.) You have the side benefit of no longer needing to compost much, if at all, as your chickens will eat almost anything from your kitchen, garden, or yard waste.

Some people find that chickens also help with maintaining or preventing ticks, moles, etc. in their immediate range. From my personal experience, the drop in population of moles in our yard seems to correspond to getting chickens, but I'm not sure how our tick numbers were affected.

You should also know that no matter how many nesting boxes you build, they will only use a couple of them. It is not unusual to see one box with 4 hens in it at a time, right next to two empty boxes. If your egg numbers suddenly drop, check three things: water supply, thief (quite likely an animal thief), or for a new nest hidden somewhere. Most likely, it is the third option.

Other Fowl

You may want to consider other barnyard fowl too, though it's often a good idea to ease into the lifestyle with chickens. As with chickens, you can sell the eggs to eat, eggs to hatch, meat, perhaps feathers, and perhaps manure.

Ducks and turkeys are pretty easy. Turkeys will actually drown themselves in their water dish when only a few days old, so be VERY careful of any standing water. Ducks on the other hand need plenty of fresh water available while they eat and for their hygiene. Most of the care and benefits are the same among all these breeds. You might also want quail (there can be a specialized market for both their eggs to eat as well as crafting), guinea hens, or even peacocks.

Which breed to choose?

LAYERS

Barred Rock (black and white striped) chickens are tough as nails, but often friendly. Typically, these hens will lay 3-5 eggs a week for the majority of the year. They lay large, light brown eggs. They will be content in a penned area, but they love to free range and are a treat to watch while they hunt insects. They are good helpers in the garden, giving you a little space but with an eagle eye for any grubs you might dig up. They are tolerant of extreme temperatures and will be very content with plenty of food and a draft-free, dry coop.

Rhode Island Red (reddish brown) chickens are also tough and hysterical to watch running around. Something about this breed running around the yard makes me think of dinosaurs for sure. They don't look at all like the scaly image I have of dinosaurs, but the way they lean forward, move their head, and turn on a dime to pounce on their prey - yup, dinosaurs.

These layers will produce an egg almost daily, providing you with large, brown eggs. Also cold tolerant, these birds are content to be penned up, but would prefer to free range for great distances. If you allow them to free range, expect that you will need to also free range search for their eggs. They lay at all times of the day from dawn to dusk (to be fair, any chicken can lay at any time of day, but some breeds are more considerate and mostly lay in the morning).

Easter Eggers/Olive Eggers (aka Americ*anas* not Americ*aunas*) These are the cool birds that lay a variety of shades of eggs - everything from a dark green to light blue, even shades of pink. I love having them mixed into my flock to add a variety of colors. They are generally tolerant of the cold. Typically, they are fluffy with small combs. This is probably because they are a variety of mixed breeds as opposed to a "true" breed themselves. They typically lay an egg every day or two for most of the year. That being said, they are my first to stop laying in the winter (shorter days).

Dual Purpose Birds

If you are just starting out or are short on space you may want to choose dual purpose birds to provide eggs and meat. However, keep in mind that once you butcher these hens, you MUST treat them differently than "typical" meat birds. You do want to let the carcass rest longer (many people will say 2-3 days at least) and you want to cook the meat slowly. Otherwise, you will have tough or rubbery meat. Because the hens are older, their muscles are more developed (unless you kept them caged), treat the meat accordingly, and you will be fine.

Rhode Island Red (reddish) are one of the most popular dual purpose breeds (just listed as a layer, because they lay so well). They are calm but friendly, and typically healthy. They eat a whole variety of foods, which many people claim leads to better tasting meat. They are bountiful egg layers, so they seem the perfect hen to have. We started with this breed and continue to always have them as 1/3-1/2 of our flock.

Astralorps (especially the black) are also a popular dual purpose hen. I have not owned these, but I am looking into getting some for our next batch since they are dual purpose. They are very friendly but likely to go broody. They are too heavy to fly well so containing them is fairly easy, although they enjoy free ranging. They produce eggs almost daily, year round.

Meat Birds

Some chickens are bred primarily for their meat. If they mature, they will produce eggs but often they are butchered before this to achieve tender meat. Typically, they are butchered between 2-4 months. Moreover, they have been bred to produce heavy weight so they become unable to walk or run very far and therefore have shorter natural lives.

If you intend to raise these birds to butcher and sell, you must check your local regulations. Usually, there are quite a few. You may find it worthwhile to invest in the equipment and certifications to butcher and package yourself. You may also find it worthwhile to hire someone certified to come to your location. Also a possibility, is bringing your live birds to someone for the butchering and packaging.

One of the most popular meat breeds are the Jersey Giants (black). These large birds grow slowly but typically are about 13 pounds by 6 months. These can be a viable dual purpose bird, but because they mature so slowly, many farmers do not choose to raise them. They can tolerate the cold and have few health problems.

Another popular breed is the Cornish Cross (white with a very small comb). These birds tend to finish at 12 pounds but in only a few months, about 8 pounds in two months. They eat ALOT because they grow so fast. Many people claim they have some of the best tasting meat. However, they need careful watching or they may grow obese and have health complications. Being so heavy, they are not very heat tolerant. These are our first choice for meat birds.

They aren't laying golden eggs but they do make money

SELLING EGGS TO EAT

It really depends on the market in your area, how much you can sell a dozen eggs for. Generally it's $3-9/dozen. We started at $3 and now we're up to $8. You want to consider what people are willing to pay but also your costs to raise these egg producing birds. It's more than just the feed, take into consideration all your costs like equipment and fencing.

You will also need to check your state and local regulations regarding selling them. Some states require a special license, some require they be washed and refrigerated, some just require they be labeled with your contact information.

As you decide how many layers you want to raise, consider how and where you will be selling your eggs:

- Friends and family
- Drive by traffic
- Farm stand
- Farmers markets
- Local stores
- Local restaurants
- CSA
- Excess can often be donated to food shelves and community kitchens.

Selling Fertilized Eggs

I don't have any personal experience in this, but I know many people who say they make good money by selling fertilized eggs. These eggs are worth even more if you can sex them. Generally, it is more successful to buy local rather than from a hatchery. You might want to corner the market with a specialized breed. Or, you might want to offer other birds such as ducks and quail as well.

You need to consider the costs of incubators and electricity. You also need to consider the risk of a power outage as the eggs have strict requirements for temperature and humidity.

As always, check your local sales regulations before investing.

Meat Birds

Selling chicken to eat typically has far more regulations than selling eggs. You will need to research this for your location.

There may be increased costs to align with regulations, but unlike layers, meat birds mature in about 8-12 weeks. It is a pretty short term investment.

To eventually increase your sales price, you can look into becoming certified organic (often difficult and costly). Because I feed my birds kitchen scraps, I can never be certified organic, as we eat more than certified, organic foods.

These chickens are actually costing me more than they are earning me!

CHICKEN FEED IS SO expensive!!!

You may find that buying feed is far more expensive than you expected. Good quality feed is, of course, more expensive, but there is a debate between pelleted or crumble. I find my girls have less mess, and therefore less waste, with pelleted. I also spring for feed designed to help with egg production. But I like to let them forage and I supplement their feed with our kitchen scraps and gardening scraps.

One of the most important things you can provide for chickens is fresh water. They always need fresh water, and frankly they aren't afraid to poop right in their water, so you may be changing it frequently. Regardless of how you feed your birds, ALWAYS provide them with plenty of water.

Foraging/Cage free/ Free range

You may choose to let your birds wander and still lock them up at night in a coop or barn for their safety. Many who do allow their chickens to wander and search for their own foods, also choose to not let them out of their coop until late morning so that they have a better chance of finding all the eggs (they will lay anywhere!).

You will have to weigh the benefits and risks of allowing your birds to run free versus keeping them in a pen. If you allow them loose to enjoy the thrill of scratching, chasing, and pecking to find their own delicacies, make sure they have plenty of places to hide from predators (from the sky or ground).

You also need to consider chicken proofing certain aspects of your property. They will see nothing wrong with hopping right up on your porch or patio and leaving behind lots of poop. They also believe that those pretty flowers and delicate garden plants are perfect for their grazing. Most of the year I am content to let the birds wander, but as my garden is just starting they are not free to roam. If they are loose, they are also supervised. Later, they eat quite a few bugs and weeds out of the garden and we coexist well, but not as the plants are tender shoots.

Also, weather and seasons will drastically affect their diet. My girls are happy to be out in the snow, but they are unable to forage much if anything and rely completely on my feeding them.

Yard and garden scraps

The girls love when I pull weeds or rake! They are more than happy to help me, but they are almost as happy if I just toss the green matter into their pen first thing in the morning. You will quickly learn which leaves they find the tastiest, and which they don't care for.

Kitchen Scraps

Our girls eat almost everything we eat. You may choose to not feed them cooked egg or chicken of course, but truthfully they will be happy to eat both. I will not feed my girls any hardboiled eggs in egg shape, I crumble it first, nor any raw eggs or egg shells. I don't want them to develop a taste for eating their eggs. There are also some scraps that they won't eat, such as onion peel, potato peels, or citrus. A friend of mine has chickens that love potato peels - go figure. Also, that lettuce that you forgot about and now it's a bit slimy (but not rotten)? Yeah, go ahead and give it to the chickens, they love it.

Community Scraps

You may be able to approach local stores and restaurants for their kitchen, deli, or produce waste. Often neighbors are happy to contribute as well. They may be quite happy to give you what would otherwise go into the dumpster. Some states have laws about this, but by clarifying that it is for animal consumption, you should be fine. Check to be sure.

I had a deal with a cafe that I sold eggs to. I sold them the eggs at a slightly lower price and in exchange they gave me selected kitchen scraps. I was able to say that I didn't want any egg shells (don't teach the girls the bad habit of enjoying raw egg) and coffee grounds (they don't eat it). It was a win for all of us.

Don't forget about other costs

Remember the initial chick or pullet cost, shelter, and feed are only some of your costs.

You also need your food and water systems, maybe a storage container for feed, possibly a light source, as well as shavings, straw*, or whatever litter you are using, egg cartons and labels if you are selling your eggs...

*Note: I have been told that you should not use hay instead of straw. Chickens may try to eat the hay and then, because of the dry texture, they are unable to completely swallow it and may develop "sour stomach". I have not verified this with a vet, but it does seem reasonable. I use shavings and therefore I don't have this issue.

Chapter 4 - Gardening

Seasonal Self-Sufficiency

Kitchen Garden

There are many people, especially beginner gardeners, who choose to have a small kitchen garden. This supplements your meals through the growing season, but does not produce surplus (unless you grow zucchini - there is always surplus zucchini). Typically, these gardens are located within easy reach of the kitchen so that one may pop out while cooking for a quick harvest to supplement a meal.

I have also heard these called salad gardens as they often include lettuce, tomato, and cucumbers, the staples of a salad, but not much else.

Some gardeners choose to include a few cut flowers and herbs, as well.

Seasonal Self-Sufficiency

This is a garden that produces more than a small kitchen garden. The kitchen (or salad) garden supplements meals. The seasonal self-sufficiency garden intends to provide almost all vegetable and herb produce for the season. We are lucky to have easy access to grocery stores and can buy plenty of herbs and non-local produce that you may not be able to produce on your homestead. I do enjoy a variety of fruits that do not grow in my climate as well as coffee. Moreover, I like to buy my sugar, flour, and such as well.

Gardening is a great time to remember that it is better to *start small and succeed before expanding*. It is very easy to pore over seed catalogs and draw out the perfect garden plot only to be overwhelmed by weather, weeds, and a lack of time. **It is ok to purchase some and be almost self-sufficient**. I would far rather buy bananas through the year than not have them available for my family simply because they will not successfully grow in my climate.

If you plan well and plans succeed, you can have a garden that produces greens early in the spring. Each week you will receive greater and greater bounty from your garden until you are buying almost no produce at the store, until the harvest begins to wan off and you begin to buy more at the store again. Fresh vegetables almost always taste more vibrant and amazing than store bought and are looked forward to through the entire year. It is absolutely an admirable goal to produce enough to meet your needs for the season, but you should never malnourish yourself, family, or animals from a stubborn desire to produce all your own food.

Once you have had a successful year of gardening I challenge you to try a new vegetable the following season. Trying new things can be great fun, and certainly lend some adventure to your meals.

Year long self-sufficiency

GOALS

The goal of producing enough produce to be self-sufficient is laudable...and huge! I would strongly encourage you to break this into stages, and not try to accomplish it all the first year.

For the sake of this section, let's assume that you have the knowledge and/or experience to preserve your bounty for after the growing season. I highly encourage you to learn these skills! Take some classes, watch videos, find a mentor, and try some easy projects to begin with. But I would never suggest to someone that they attempt a huge garden and a year's worth of preservation for the first year. There are so many scenarios that can fail these plans, Start small, succeed, and expand. I have been gardening and preserving almost my entire life, and I do not try to be entirely self-sufficient. I have neither sufficient storage space, nor the time and money to produce enough for a well balanced diet. I do grow and preserve; we eat our products year round, but they supplement our bought groceries.

As you become more experienced not only in your own skills, but also what your gardens can produce, you can be more reliant upon yourself for self-sufficiency. Always have a contingency plan though. There will be crop failures. There will be accidents of failed freezers or collapsed shelves that will ruin the best of your plans.

Selling Your Surplus

JUST AS LIKELY, MAYBE more likely than a crop failure is a crop that just goes crazy. It's great to freeze, can, and give away your surpluses, but you may want to sell some as well. Once you know how your garden typically performs, you may choose to purposely overplant in order to have surplus.

Fresh or Added Value

THERE ARE TWO MAIN categories of how to sell your surplus crops (or almost any product: meat, honey, syrup,...). Do you want to sell them fresh (picked and washed, or picked, washed, and weighed) or do you want to process and sell them?

As always, check your insurance and local regulations regarding the sale of fresh produce, frozen produce, baked goods, and canned goods. You may be able to sell your little bit of extra under minimal cottage laws, or your area may have very strict regulations. Always be prepared to tell any buyer and/or inspector about your gardening practices and your kitchen practices. Fresh produce may require a certified washing station and soil/water tests. Prepared goods (baked or preserved) you most likely need a label with your contact information and ingredients, and maybe more information. Check the local requirements.

I have sold both, the fresh extra produce (who doesn't end up with extra zucchini?!?) as well as value added. Because I don't want to deal with annually certifying a scale, I never sell by weight. Instead, I sell at a set price such as $.50 each or 3 for $1. I also sometimes sell by the bag (still not by weight). I allow my customers to see all that is offered and to choose their own, my prices are clearly marked. This works for me as I don't sell a lot of produce. I also sometimes pick and sell wild, foraged berries. Again, I sell by the container/bag not by the weight.

More often, I sell the produce used in something. For a while I was completely overrun with squashes and cucumbers - I'm sure I will be again this summer. So I was bringing them to sell fresh at the market and I was pickling them. Plus we ate a ton. I also shredded and froze a bunch of the zucchini for me to bake with this winter. In January, we're ready for zucchini bread and muffins again, about August we are sick of them. These particular crops allowed us to eat them fresh/seasonally, plus store for us for the rest of the year (frozen and pickled), and to sell the extra (fresh and pickled). I happened to have a booth placement near another baker last summer, so I did not usually sell baked goods. I may this year.

The general practice is that the more labor put into an item means the greater the price. Plus, adding more containers and ingredients often increases the price. So the cost of buying two cucumbers is drastically different than buying a jar of pickles even though the amount of actual cucumber may be about the same. You may find that you don't have time to pickle and preserve, or you may find the best use of your time is to double a batch of pickles specifically for the purpose of selling the second batch. You need to find what works for you in terms of supply, time, and enjoyment, then factor in cost vs profit.

I also really prefer "set it and forget it" type of value adds. I make our own applesauce, it's super easy. I (usually) peel the apples, core them, slice them, add a tiny bit of water and forget about them for hours in the crockpot. I may or may not blend them. Two batches of this I can mix in the crockpot with some sugar and cinnamon and suddenly I have apple butter. My total work time is quite short, but I can sell a 1/2 pint for $8 easily. The apples are a minimal cost, the electricity is minimal, the cinnamon is minimal, sugar varies but I stock up when it's on sale, so that's cheap. My greatest expense is the jars. Pickles are easy, too. You make a bunch as the vegetables come into season and you can store them until you're ready to sell, even if it's months later. If you do decide to try your hand at selling value added items, I suggest seeing what others are selling. You may want to copy the most popular, but find some unique items of your own as well. For example, as far as I know, I was the only one selling dilly carrots last year at the farmers markets which was a great niche, but many of us sold pickled beets and always sold out. Many, many people sold dill pickles and dilly beans, so I didn't usually carry those unless I had a jar or two surplus from our own-use batches.

What if you're not into vegetables, or your soil just isn't conducive to that? That's ok, there are plenty more options. First, you might be selling potted plants. Starts (the seedlings that will be transplanted into gardens) are HUGEly popular in the spring. Potted flowers are popular all season long but especially around holidays. Cut flowers are gorgeous and popular, but make sure it is feasible just in case they don't all sell.

You can't just hold onto them until next week like you can many other products. Maybe you can dry them for crafts or maybe you donate them to a nursing home. There are plenty of uses for unsold cut flowers.

Herbs are another great option. Growing, cutting, and selling them fresh, growing and selling potted herbs, or even, growing, drying, and perhaps grinding them makes for fantastic sales. Value added herb products are a great seller in crafts fairs and farmers markets. Everything from teas to flavored salts, infused oils to bath ingredients, even many sewn projects from heating pads to cat toys. There may be more regulations as you move into bath and body products, especially if you make any sort of health or healing claim.

Where to sell is just as important as what to sell

IF YOU HAVE A CERTIFIED or licensed kitchen you can probably sell out of state. I work under cottage laws and can only sell in-state. This means that I don't attempt to sell my kitchen/garden goods online. (Eggs are probably the same regulations, but I just don't even want to consider how to ship them!) So I choose to sell by WOM (word of mouth) and at three farmers markets. Many people have great luck with a farmstand or little store on their property, as well. We don't have that much traffic going by, nor do I want a bunch of people wondering about my property, so we do not have our own stand. Again, local regulations may come into play for how you can sell.

You need to consider how much extra you will have and want to sell, what the regulations are, insurance requirements, and where you should sell. You also need to consider storage. What doesn't immediately sell, needs to be kept food safe and also appealing. By this I mean, I have no problem keeping it food safe, but anything stored more than a few weeks in my house often seems to collect a few stray dog hairs. No one wants to buy a jar of pickles with a piece of dog hair on it, even if there is absolutely no contamination. It's just not appealing.

You might have dreams of fantastic sales of fresh produce and value added deliciousness, but this is another aspect that I urge you to start small, succeed, and then expand. In fact, you might even want to start by using your first year's surplus as gifts, and as you give them away tell people that you intend to sell them next year. You may find that to be your best WOM marketing.

You have a world of possibilities when it comes to gardening. Find what you enjoy and what is profitable and go from there.

CSAs are Community Supported Agriculture.

CSAS HAVE A VARIETY of organization and looks, but most often they are associated with crop or animal shares. I do not recommend anyone attempt this their first year. Actually, I would recommend gathering several years of experience, first. Once you do begin, have plenty of back up plans. There will be droughts, pests, funguses, crop failures or ugly fruits, market drops, illnesses and injuries, etc. You will need to plant extra and you will need to have money set aside in case you need to offer any sort of refund (offering credits is often better). If you enjoy gardening or animal care, this can be an amazing way to bring in income and basically feed your family for free (aside from your time and labor).

Specialty Crops

SPECIALTY CROPS MAY be exactly the niche you need to market, or it may be your inspiration and happiness. Either way, research what you need before buying anything. Consider climate, space, fertilizers, water, mulch, time, supplies, seeds/seedlings, storage,...

Specialty crops is a simple sounding term that can cover a great deal. It may be simply that you choose to grow heritage tomatoes, it may be that you grow hemp, it may be that you have decided to grow unusual plants (to your area) like loofahs and lavender to compliment a bath and body line.

Find something that interests you, then see what the market is. See if there are additional ways that you can use the product if your sales don't meet your expectations. Go for it. Become the expert. Enjoy it!

Chapter 5 - Hunting, fishing, trapping, foraging

CHOOSING TO BE OUT in the woods, by the water, in a field, at an ocean, or anywhere out and about is amazing for so many reasons. It is good for your heart and your spirit to be out in nature and immersed in those energies. The goal is to take your benefits from the natural surroundings without causing damage to them or impairing someone else's ability to enjoy nature. Largely this is based on respect.Go outside, absorb the good, AND gain some income!

Safety and Respect

Always when you're in the woods or fields you should be safe. You need to be safe and aware of your surroundings and what may change, but also be safe in how you act. Let's break this down a little:

You need to be sure that you are making safe choices by letting someone know where you expect to be and when you expect to return. Now to be fair, I don't do that around the house when I'm out picking berries, but if I'm hiking in a good distance somewhere, I would let someone know my expectations (where I'll be, how long I think it will be, whether I'll be alone). More than likely this will never really matter, but you do it for the times that something goes seriously wrong and help needs to be sent.

Next, you need to make sure you know how to safely handle any equipment you bring with you. This might be as simple as having your boots broken in some before walking in 5 miles and having the sole give way from the boot itself, or it might be knowing how to safely use your brand new flyfishing gear, or that handy rifle you expect to shoot big game with. Not only do you need to completely understand and be comfortable with the equipment, but you need to know how to use it safely so you: 1, don't endanger any human, and 2: so you don't wound and cause an animal needless suffering.

There are plenty of safety courses when it comes to using equipment. Find a mentor or take a course (or both). It is worth it.

Finally, you also want to consider the impact of your actions on others. You never want to put yourself in needless danger causing others to be hurt or waste their energy to help you. You never want to ruin an area for others or destroy the plants or animals of an area. I fully support hunting, but only if the animal will be used. I hate killing an animal (or bird or reptile,...) for the sake of just killing it. Eat the meat, use the hide, whatever, just use it. Kill it cleanly and use it. Appreciate the life you took to benefit your own. (I feel the same about farm-raised meat.) The same is true for what you forage. Opinions vary whether you should be harvesting only 10% of an area or up to 40%. Ultimately, it depends on the abundance of the supply, the length of time for it to grow, and how many others (human or otherwise) also need it. Learn how to properly harvest mushrooms for example so that they can grow back another year. Leave enough honey in the bees' nest that the swarm can survive (preferably thrive) the winter. Tap a maple tree carefully so as not to introduce diseases. Never lay a trap where you cannot easily and quickly check it, and be sure that nothing unsuspected is caught.

You do need to be careful of other environmental factors. There might be gorgeous dandelions beside the road, but those dandies may have been sprayed with all sorts of pesticides and road chemicals. Maybe those wash off, maybe they are completely absorbed into the plant. Next to the road might not be the best place to harvest wine-making supplies.

Respect the natural balances of the wilderness and work within them. Respect nature. Respect others using the resources (human or otherwise). It comes down to observing and respect.

Filling your Pantry

IT IS PERFECTLY LEGITIMATE to fill your pantry and freezer with foods that you hunt, trap, fish, and forage. It is not ok to waste what you take. As a realist I know that there are unforeseen events, but you should be taking every precaution and using every bit of education you can to avoid any waste.

Following a successful hunt (my son's), we carefully clean the meat, cut it into steaks or stew meat and freeze. The scraps that we don't find pleasurable to eat (fat, etc) we mix in with the dog's food. Our goal is to use as much as we possibly can.

Many people consider stocking up with the meat they hunt and trap, and the fish they catch, but they forget about other ways to forage and fill their larders. One of the first things we hunt in the spring is actually foraging for fiddlehead ferns. These are delectable sauteed in butter. Most people add some garlic, I like just salt and pepper. We always eat them fresh although I have considered finding enough to freeze and can. Likewise, I love spending hot summer days out collecting berries. To be fair many of these are eaten right away plain or in some sort of berry cobbler, but others I freeze for winter muffins and pancakes. With enough berries I can also make jams. I pick apples to can applesauce and apple butter. I may use the apple sauce plain, or bake with it, or even mix it later with other flavors to dehydrate and make fruit roll-ups. My children seldom like to eat plain wild apples, preferring the big, juicy, store bought ones, but that's ok.

There are plenty of mushrooms available year round to stock your pantry with, either eating them fresh or drying them for winter sauces and soups. Some examples of other lesser known items that can be foraged are birch bark or oak to grind and make flour, cattails as a tuber similar to potatoes, and plenty of needles and twigs to make teas. Year round there are foraging possibilities, but you need to explore, and maybe do quite a bit of research, before you truly understand what is available on your property and surrounding areas. The sweetest foraging might be if you're lucky enough to find a wild hive of honey, or here in the northeast, we have glorious maple trees for sap to be boiled into maple syrup. There are other saps that can be used too, see what you have.

Remember to harvest responsibly so that others (human or animals) may also harvest there AND that you do not destroy the area for future harvest.

It depends on the local laws whether you can also take home roadkill. While you might not be comfortable with the idea of taking home a dead raccoon to eat, a deer that was killed instantly by an SUV might sound more appealing. I think it's better for the animal to be used than just to rot on the side of the road.

Legalities

HOPEFULLY THE LAWS and policies in your area allow you to harvest what you want, when you want, off of your land. This tends to be largely true, but there are some regulations to look into. You may find there are other regulations when you go on other's private land (rule of thumb is to be respectful and ask the property owner(s) first, regardless of what the law says) or even public land. For example, many state and federal land will allow you to forage year round, they may allow you to hunt, you may even be allowed to harvest wood/timber for personal use (but there are usually rules about how much and that it must be pulled out in a non-motorized manner). The possibilities are pretty endless. Strive for good relations with your neighbors as you find the prime locations. Maybe you can set up some bartering, find what works for you.

On the flip side of this, you may find that you have no interest in hunting, for example, but love to forage. Perhaps your land is prime for hunting big game. You should check your insurance to see what your coverage is for allowing others to hunt on your land. I absolutely believe in sharing the bounties of the land (and water and air) with everyone, but I want to keep my family safe, my property respected, and not be sued for their own silliness. Check to see what requirements there are. Also, if someone asks to hunt on your property, it is entirely fair to say, "Sure, but can we barter?" and suggest a deal that they give you a couple steaks or allow you to forage on their land in exchange for hunting on yours.

Guiding

ONCE YOU HAVE LEARNED the prime hunting, fishing, trapping, and foraging spots around you, there is a good chance that you also know fantastic canoe/kayaking routes and hiking ways. You may want to consider becoming a guide. Maybe you bring people on wildlife tours, or offer to lead photography students. Maybe you actually bring hunting tours about. This might be another stream of income for you that ties into your love of nature, even if you are "tagged-out" (tagging-out refers to having used all of the state issued tags for your personal hunting each year, there tend to be limits of how many deer, turkey, or moose, etc that can be harvested in a given season by any one hunter.)

You can choose what to offer and whether to allow killing as a part of your services. Maybe you even take it a step further and include days in the woods/on the water and evening classes on how to prepare the harvest. You can create a package any way you want within the law. BUT AGAIN check insurance. There are plenty of opportunities to be a guide, but you absolutely want to be insured.

Value Added (selling bait, sewing leather/fur hats, etc)

JUST AS GARDENING HAS a direct benefit (fresh produce) it also offers income through value-added products (increasing the value by preparing the produce into another more expensive product). What you find in the wilderness is no different. Let's think hunting and trapping - you can use the pelts (furs) for a variety of sewn projects from mittens to jackets; you can use the antlers and bones for a variety of carved products, furniture, or even dog training; if you have the skillset you can even save the sinew for projects. Bird feathers may have some uses, but there are a surprising number of federal regulations regarding the sale or transport of wild bird feathers. While it would seem a great stream of income to use found feathers for art, jewelry, even fly fishing, the regulations may impact you.

I already mentioned that I forage fruits and berries. A simple value add is pickles or jams. But one could also dehydrate the berries to be added to foods like oatmeal or eaten plain.

Foraging for pretty stones, acorns, and wood pieces can lead to amazing craft supplies. You can sell these directly, as DIY kits, or the finished craft. The kit is worth more than just the supplies, but the greatest value-add is the completed craft. Fairy gardens and fairy houses are still popular. While you are checking trap lines it's easy to collect some pretty rocks, small twigs, and plenty of nuts. Then you can set aside the materials until you're ready and craft away later. Pine needles are another great resource. Collect them when it's convenient for you, spread them out to dry if you'll be storing them, then weave them into baskets when you're ready. The fancier the basket, generally the more expensive it is, and some go for $1,000 easily!

You can certainly go out and dig for bait each day and sell it, but it might be worth a corner of your yard or garage to build a worm farm (two totes are all you need). The worms can be used for your own bait, plus you can sell the bait to other fishermen. Moreover, worm castings and worm "tea" are fantastic for your garden (you might not want it on houseplants, if the PH is just a little off, it could be smelly). So are the worms, if you get sick of having them or want to be done at the end of summer. If you decided that worms are easy you might even want to try your hand at other types of worms and insects. As a value add, instead of fresh you could dry these tasty treats to be sold as animal treats. In theory, you could sell them for human consumption, but I'm sure there is strict licensing and generally there are enough people with pet reptiles and chickens to make pet snacks completely lucrative and far easier.

Find what you enjoy about outdoors and think about how you can expand it just a touch to be an extra income stream. It can be just a trickle, but if it pays for itself, then it's probably worth it.

Chapter 6 - Make money with your hobby

You always need a way to relax and have fun. Don't ruin your hobby by turning it into a business.

It's one thing to be straight out in the months of March and April making a product for Mother's day and being absolutely sick of it by April 30th, not wanting to see it again until at least August. It is another thing to continuously dread the activity that has previously been an enjoyment.

Balance is usually the key.

You may find that teaching your skill adds a whole new level of enjoyment. Also, it's really nice when people want to buy our products and even better when they tell us how much they enjoyed them.

Share your skills

IT IS NOT JUST AN INTROVERT extrovert battle to decide whether to focus sharing your hobby online or in person, or both.

You must find where you are most comfortable, or where you can fake it.

You must find where your most interested audience is located.

Teaching in person or online

(SEE MORE ON THIS LATER in this lecture)

Different types of classes have different needs which is just as important as where and how you feel comfortable. These are just as important to consider as is social distancing during a pandemic.

However, you also want to consider your audience and what they are comfortable with. Some introverts will not attend an in-person class. Some people love the social in-person classes. You might want to consider recording all or portions of your in-person teaching to create an online version.

Workshop style in-person

SOME CLASSES ARE BEST taught in a small workshop setting in person. Inherently, these classes have limited "seating" availability. Generally a how-to type of class, and certainly one involving animal care, should be in a small setting.

These can be informal like a [activity of choice] & sip at a local cafe or pub, or more formal at a community center or museum. Either way, you need to figure all your costs, plus profit, and then divide that by your small audience.

Lecture in-person

THIS CAN BE LARGE OR small in person. This might be at a school or community center, or it might be at a university or town hall. In this case your "seating" numbers can be much higher, but you are limited at being able to do anything hands-on. There are some creative ways around this with activity bags at check in that can be worked on at one's seat, but large groups mean you cannot individually help people. This is better for teaching via anecdotes and video projection. Something like a lecture on foraging is ideal for this with plenty of photos to be projected and your own foraging adventure stories. Quite likely the cost per student will be lower as you don't have individual supplies, but you may have greater overhead in terms of space rental.

Again, you may want to consider recording this event to then show online.

Online self-paced

THIS IS THE KIND OF course that I tend to take and is the style of this book.

You post all of your lectures and activities in advance. The student then works through them as they have the time. The advantages to this is that it can fit any kind of schedule and is evergreen (can be done at any season). The downside is that you miss the interactions between students via discussion. You also miss having support groups on Facebook or other platforms that help pump up the excitement.

Online scheduled

THIS TYPE OF COURSE is one that you can promote in a variety of groups and have countdown excitement. There are many courses in this style promoted on Social Media all the time.

The downside is that there are students who will not commit to completing the entire course in a set time, or who are scared to commit. It is really hard to teach a time consuming hobby like knitting this way, as projects can fall behind.

The upside is that you can have a very active discussion in the class and in supporting social media groups building up excitement and during the course supporting each other. I have done workshops in this style and I love sharing and learning with others going through the same material.

Selling items in person or online

WHETHER TO SELL IN person or online really depends on a few things:

> Can what you are selling be reasonably shipped? (For example I can sell eggs in person but I am not shipping them.)
>
> Regulations by city, state, and federal. (For example, I can only sell baked goods within my state by my current license.)
>
> What fees you are willing to pay? Almost any venue will take a fee or commission for you to sell on, at, or through them. A farmers market will often have an annual fee, and % commission. Craft fairs will often have a vendor fee/booth space fee. A brick and mortar store will usually charge a commission. Online platforms may have listing fees and/or commissions.
>
> Sales tax. Collect it and remit it in person. Online platforms may collect and remit for you - be sure whether they are or if you need to.
>
> Do you enjoy the social interaction or would you like a buffer between you and the buyer?
>
> Are your items personalized so in-person sales are not feasible?

I offer both options. At farmers markets and craft fairs I can sell eggs and baked goods, as well as crafts. Online and on commission, I sell only crafts.

Offering services in person or online

THIS REALLY DEPENDS on the service you are offering. Clearly hoof trimming is not an online service, but editing can be either in-person or online.

Regardless of which you choose, you should make sure that you have the expectations and commitments IN WRITING. For the best legal protection you want a full contract drawn up, but this may be unnecessary for some projects. I have set up some services via text, with someone I know that I have good communication with.

Depending on the service you offer you may want to go through a platform like Fiverr or Upwork. This gives you some protection in receiving your money, and makes the buyers more confident in hiring you. It also gives you a buffer in personal contact information. These sites have a rating system too, so you can build up your reputation, while seeing feedback on your potential buyers.

Farmers Market Vs Craft Fair

DIFFERENT PEOPLE THRIVE in different situations, and your niche (your place, your buying audience) may be better suited to one venue over another. Personally I enjoy both Farmers Markets and Craft Fairs, but you may find a preference for one over another. There are pros and cons to each. I could reinvent the wheel here and write a whole new lecture on the advantages and disadvantages of certain venues. However, this is a subject that I have written about in our blog several times - SecondTimeAroundHomestead.com.

Here's an excerpt from, Farmers Market vs Craft Fair - Which is Right For You?[1]

I quickly concluded my own little farm stand would be ideal, but we just don't have the traffic passing by that I would need. And, for now, I like not having people at my house.

---

1. https://secondtimearoundhomestead.com/2020/03/02/farmers-markets-vs-craft-fairs-what-is-the-right-venue-for-you/

Three big things affect your initial plans. First and foremost is the quantity (while maintaining quality) of supply. You do not want to overcommit, so make sure you have the time to make, the necessary materials, and the room to store your supply. Second, you need to consider your time. Do you have the time not only to produce your materials but also tie up every Saturday for a Farmers Market or would you rather do a three day craft fair and then have a break? Lastly, you need to consider the audience. There is absolutely no point to having plenty of amazing products if you are going to waste your time trying to sell to people who aren't really interested in your product. The final considerations are fees, set-up, travel, and general impact upon your life.

Time can be a benefit or a challenge to us all. It ties directly to quantity and quality of product as well. You MUST consider how much time you need to create or prep your products before ever getting near a sales table, plus how long it takes you to put up (and take down) a good display, travel time, and time you might want with your family or doing other things.

Audience is the one I am stuck on right now, the repeat buyer versus seasonality of my product. If I sold gourmet fudge, then there is a good chance that I could have repeat customers every week at a Farmer's Market. But since I focus on selling market tote bags[2]*, what are the chances of repeat buyers every week? I expand my line with other products, some of which are seasonal like winter hats, these would also not be a weekly repeat. So the question is do I have enough variety that I could make enough sales every single week at a Farmer's Market or am I better off at a variety of Craft shows?*

Also, an excerpt from, Ready For Your First Farmers Market?[3]

First, your background information

BEFORE YOU START SELLING there are several steps to do. Luckily, I did these last year. Do your research on when, where, and what times the markets are. Find out what fees they require. Are there annual memberships and a fee each week? Find out what they currently offer for wares and if you will have a niche. Find out how successful the market typically is. Find out how often there are other events (festivals, live music, construction, good and bad factors) that may affect the attendance. Think about how you will handle all the seasons and types of weather. Lastly, find out what licenses, fees, and labeling

2. *https://www.etsy.com/VermontelfsHomestead/listing/747941111/eco-friendly-red-and-black-horse?utm_source=Copy&utm_medium=ListingManager&utm_campaign=Share&utm_term=so.lmsm&share_time=1583194112884*

3. https://secondtimearoundhomestead.com/2021/06/03/ready-for-your-first-farmers-market/

requirements there are for you as a vendor and your products locally, state, and federally. ...

Second, choose your products

SO TRUTHFULLY I HAVE a ton of hobbies that could lead to sales at a local farmers market. But I don't want so much diversity that I am always running out of the products and am unreliable to my customers. ...

Third, prepare your space and supplies

BEFORE I ACTUALLY HAD the phone conversation to fully commit to the weekly market (but after being invited this year) I hopped on Amazon to replace our pop-up tent canopy and to order a folding table. I even splurged and ordered a canopy with sides to keep me comfy on the rainy days and this fall. I have old laundry bottles and the like to fill with wet sand (maybe just water this weekend) which I'll beautify at some point. Meanwhile I am making arrangements to borrow a table and canopy in case mine don't arrive before Saturday. You want to draw up a full list of ***EVERYTHING*** *you need. Keep the list to double check that you have packed everything before you leave. ...*

You have fantastic skills - share them!

TEACHING YOUR SKILLS is not only a great way to make money, but also to network and share ideas.

However, you want to consider a few things before you have your first class:

Location

Your cost and preparation and participants' costs and expectations.

Short term vs long term vs series, seasonal vs evergreen.

Location

IT MIGHT BE EASIEST to teach your given subject right on your property, but you need to check your infrastructure and your liabilities.

First and foremost, you need the right insurance coverage.

Second, you need enough parking, bathroom space, workspace and chairs, etc.

Third, you must be ADA accessible and be able to safely have a group of people "wandering" about.

Fourth, you must consider poor weather and back up plans. Power outages? Ice storm? Crazy heatwave? Water failure?

Fifth, meals or foods. You must have safe storage and preparation. You need to be aware of food allergies. You want people to be comfortable.

Sixth, I'm writing this in the middle of the Covid pandemic. I would be remiss to not mention the safety and regulations regarding groups and social interactions.

Unless you already regularly have groups to your property and are set up for it, I recommend finding a host location and offering workshops there. That location then is responsible for most of the legal issues and infrastructure. Essentially you arrive, set up, teach, socialize, pack up, and leave.

You still must find a hosting location that is suitable to your class. I don't know that the front room of a cafe is right for demonstrating barnyard fowl health care... Consider both the space and your audience.

There are many, many locations that you can use. Local schools and colleges may have space, but also libraries and community centers. Cafes, bars, pubs, etc often offer "[Workshop] and Sip" events. Museums may host classes and events also, as well as festivals.

Your cost and preparation & your participants' costs and expectations

PRICING CAN BE DIFFICULT to figure.

First, I recommend that you research what others are charging for a class similar to what you are thinking about. What do they offer? What is the length? What is the price? How many attendees per class?

Second, take your research and compare that to what you were thinking. Are they similar? Completely different? Are you comfortable with the similarities and differences?

Third, figure out your total cost for: the location, any licenses or special insurances, special equipment/rentals, material cost, food/drinks, transportation, hotel stay, and your time (before, during, after), advertising. Then divide this by your ideal number of students (5? 10? 25?). This number is the minimum cost of your class per person. Can you reasonably charge more? What will you do if you don't have a full class attendance? What is your cancellation policy?

Now look at it from the students' point of view. What do they get out of the course as a whole? For each class? What makes your teaching worth the entry price? It is ALWAYS better to under-promise and overdeliver, but it helps if everyone has similar expectations. Be sure it is clear what is included in the entry fee and what they need to provide. Make sure they understand the pricing, especially if there are tiers. Make your cancellation policy clear.

Short term vs long term vs series, seasonal vs evergreen

CONSIDER WHAT SORT of teaching you want to do. Are you interested in offering this as a one-time workshop? Are you thinking every Wednesday for 7 weeks? Or maybe as a drop-in type space and mentorship?

Consider when you want to offer this.

If you are leading a workshop about seedlings, you probably are only offering this in the spring and early summer, not the fall. Likewise, Christmas wreaths are definitely not a July hobby.

If you are teaching something that isn't seasonal (aka evergreen) you can offer your classes anytime you like. But, you want to consider what is best for you. Maybe even in your busiest time of year you can devote an entire Saturday to an 8 hour class. Maybe you want to avoid harvest season as you are out straight between the gardens and canning. Maybe half your income is earned through lambing season, in which case, that is not when you want to be teaching.

Plan for what works best for you. Consider not the time of the actual class but the actual class plus all the prep work and any follow up. Start small and learn from the experience. Make your second one even more successful. Decide if this is a good use of your time and energy. If not, if you don't enjoy it, don't do it anymore. If so, expand your audience and teach more.

Our Homestead's Recipes

This third book, of our favorite recipes, fills the gap of everyday survival that you may need. Some weeks are so busy you just want easy meals. This book is the resource for simple, quick meals that are family tested. These recipes have passed the test of all six of us, except seafood - only half the family likes that. You just can't please everyone all the time, that's why sandwiches and cereal were invented.

I enjoy baking some of the time, in fact I sell baked goods through the local farmers market, but I get so tired of having to cook dinner every.single.day. Some days, by the time 5 o'clock rolls around I hardly even have the energy to cook a decent meal. When my life is organized I have some freezer meals prepped, or at least can throw together ingredients in the crock pot around noon to save my sanity around 5pm!

These recipes are not gourmet, but they are real. These are recipes that we use, and have used since our children were little (they are voracious teens now). Most of these can be put together with minimal work and with ingredients that I typically stock (seafood is an exception).

Tips and Tricks

- Whenever possible, do twice the work at once. In other words, brown up twice the amount of ground beef you need for tacos so that it is already prepped when you make pasta later in the week.

- Make double batches of soups and casseroles and freeze the second.

- It's not lazy to buy coleslaw mix, rotisserie chicken etc. You need to consider the extra cost of that prepared food vs the worth of your time and energy. I often buy the shredded coleslaw mix, then add the bottled dressing and have it ready to serve in about a minute flat. Completely worth the extra money on buying it pre-shredded. Probably worth more, as I wouldn't actually need full heads of cabbage shredded and then it would be wasted (or fed to the chickens).

- Not all freezer meals are precooked. I like to prep and freeze meals too. For example I can slice and freeze peppers and onions into one bag, chicken strips in another, then add to a gallon size bag with tortillas and fajita seasoning. I take it out in the am and that night I can sautee up the meat and veggies with almost no effort.

- Buy meat when it's on sale and package it ready to cook. I may buy chicken when it's on sale, douse with the marinade and freeze. When it thaws, the meat will soak up that marinade and be ready to grill or broil. If you have a vacuum sealer, this works even better.

Slow Cooker

I love using the slow cooker for three reasons:

1. It's easy - most recipes require minimal chopping, then you dump it, stir it (maybe), set it, and forget it.
2. The clean up is also super easy. You use very few pieces to prep the meal. You can serve it directly from the slow cooker (maybe you have another pot with a side, and a salad bowl) and that can go directly in the dishwasher.
3. It cooks itself without heating up the kitchen - perfect for summer. Also it cooks itself anywhere, allowing me to use the stove for other things like pickling or baking.

All crock pots or slow cookers vary in temperatures and cook times. I tend to do our very full crockpot for 6-8 hours on low. If I am in a rush (ie, starting late) I may run it for an hour or two at a higher temperature and then finish long and lower. Check about ½ way through to see if you should adjust your temperature. Resist the urge to check it frequently, these are designed to run covered for a long period of time.

Chuck roast

SUPER EASY! CHEAP AND fairly healthy.

Ingredients:

1-2 chuck roasts or "pot roasts". Sometimes I use one large roast, sometimes I have two small ones on top of each other.

Enough broth to cover the roast (almost any flavor of broth will work).

Potatoes, Carrots, and onion based on your preferences. (We use a small onion, a lot of potato and a fair amount of carrots.)

Salt and pepper to taste

Yellow mustard and ground horseradish (optional)

1. Season your meat with salt and pepper. Add other seasonings if you like such as garlic powder, but the beauty of this dish is the simple flavors coming together.
2. Plop that meat into the crockpot, and then add water to just barely cover the meat.*
3. Peel and chop onion into large chunks and drop into the crockpot, trying to avoid clumps.
4. Peel and chop the carrots into bite size pieces and drop in the crock pot around the edge
5. Peel and chop the potatoes in bite-size chunks or wedges, then drop in the crockpot.**
6. Season the veggies with a little more salt and pepper.

Your meat should become tender, as well as the carrots and potatoes.

When fully cooked the meat should break apart with a fork, but you can certainly serve it as soon as the center is fully cooked.

My family likes to mash up the veggies on their plate with some of the broth. We then serve with yellow mustard and ground horseradish on the meat. Served with warm bread or rolls is hard to beat.

*If you are using a small roast, you may want to fill the sides with veggies and then cover the meat with broth. Ultimately, make sure the meat is covered by liquid for the cooking process.

**Try to cover the potatoes with the water, or the ones with an uncovered surface may turn gray. This doesn't affect the taste, but does look less appealing.

Corn Chowder

DUE TO THE CREAM, THE soup may separate when frozen. Try to make what you can eat in a day or two or mix really well after thawing and heating. This is a soup we enjoy often in the fall and winter.

Ingredients:

2c of broth (vegetable or chicken both work well)

1 small onion

1-2c cubed potato

1c corn

Other veggies as you like (I have successfully added broccoli, mushrooms, shredded carrots, and celery)

½c leftover pork cubed and/or a few pieces of leftover bacon crumbled

3-4T butter

1-2c milk or cream

Salt and pepper as desired

Dried parsley if desired

1. Saute your diced onion and any other crisp vegetables (carrots, celery, etc.). Then dump in a crockpot. (You can skip the sauteing, but it tastes just a little better if you complete this step.)
2. Add the potatoes. You can also use some leftover mashed potatoes if you like.
3. Add any other vegetables.
4. Add pork, then broth.
5. Salt and pepper to taste, then add butter.
6. Cook for several hours until potatoes are tender.
7. About 10-20 minutes before you will serve, add milk or cream. I use light cream.
8. Check the seasoning. Serve once the soup is hot again after

adding the cream.

Sissy's Beef stew

(THIS RECIPE IS USED in two Kindle Vellas: my own Through the Gate and Dom Sabasti's The Charred Axe)

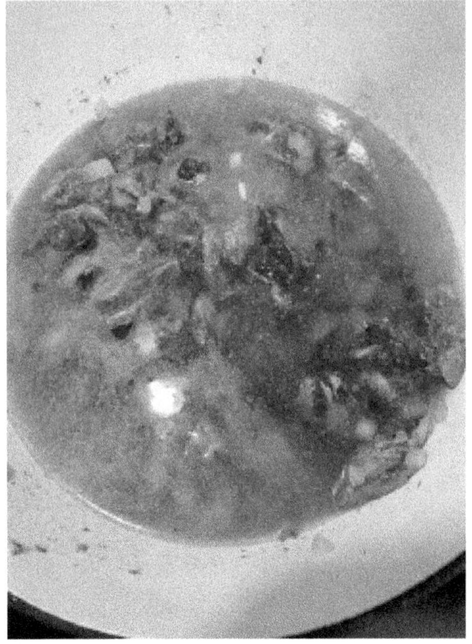

Ingredients:
stew beef 1-3 pounds (venison substitutes well)
French Onion (dried) soup mix
potatoes & carrots
mushrooms
salt and very little pepper to taste (the soup mix has seasoning so do not season more until near the end)
water or broth

1. Peel, chop, and dump in carrots and potatoes.
2. Dump in chopped up stew beef (the butcher usually provides it in the bite size pieces if you want).

3. Shake onion soup mix over the meat.
4. Add sliced mushrooms or other veggies.
5. Add water or broth as desired. We tend to want our stew thick so I do not add a lot of water, just enough to mostly cover everything. Other people like it more "soup-like" and add more liquid.
6. About ½ way through the cook time, if you are available, stir the ingredients to mix the seasoning through.
7. About an hour before serving, stir up and taste. Add salt and pepper as desired.

We like this served with bread and butter. Homemade bread is the best, but store bought works just fine too. A later section of this series has our recipe for Beer Bread which is super easy to make. Sometimes we serve it over rice, instead.

I can usually get photos of this while I'm cooking it, but by the time it's ready to eat, there's no time for photos-only eating! So this is just after I added the meat and a little stock following sauteing the onion.

Casseroles

Most casseroles can be made as a double batch to serve the first and freeze the second. I would recommend using the frozen casserole within two months. Make sure that any pasta or rice is completely covered by sauce or liquid so that it doesn't dry out. Make sure you completely seal/cover the casserole so that it doesn't dry out or collect ice crystals. I bought some cheap metal pans to use in my freezer as they don't break and leave my glass pans free. I cover them with aluminum foil, which is easy to write on (contents, cook temp and cook time) with a permanent marker.

If you are really lucky, you can move the pan from the freezer to the oven in the morning, set your oven to come on at a particular time at a particular temperature and it will cook dinner for you with almost no effort. Mine also has a "cook time" setting so it will also shut off on its own alleviating stress of being delayed and burning the house down.

American Shepherd's Pie

"REAL" SHEPHERD'S PIE is made with ground lamb, pork, etc, but Americanized Shepherd's Pie is made using ground beef. This recipe is beef based. The techniques would be the same, but the seasonings altered for other meat.

Ingredients:

1-2 pounds of ground beef

½ an onion or 1t dried onion flakes

2 cans of creamed corn

potatoes (I use a lot of potatoes because I like a thick layer of mashed potato)

butter,

cream or milk

parsley

salt and pepper to taste

1. Begin by browning and draining the ground beef, while peeling, slicing and boiling the potatoes
2. This is actually a quick meal to throw together, but it freezes really well, so if you can double the batch, even if you use a disposable tinfoil pan, do it. Some other day you can pull the pan from the freezer, slide it in the oven, bake, and be done. Cook time is a little longer if frozen and I tend to raise the temperature about 25-50 degrees.
3. When the beef is browned and the grease poured off, add finely chopped onion and cook for a few more minutes. Add salt and pepper to taste. If you are using dried onion, you do not need any additional cooking time, just season to taste with the dried onion, salt, and pepper.
4. Spread meat in the pan, then top with the cans of cream corn. The corn will be a fairly thin layer.
5. When potatoes are soft, drain, then mash with butter to taste. I use my hand mixer to do this to make them smooth really quickly. Mix in cream or milk, salt, pepper, and parsley to taste.
6. Spoon the mashed potatoes over the corn. Try to spread it evenly and to the edges (this helps seal in any liquids and prevents it from bubbling over).

Lasagna

I USED TO THINK THAT lasagna was terribly difficult to make. Then I learned that it isn't so hard and my whole world changed. This freezes well as long as all of the pasta is covered by sauce. Otherwise, the noodles get too hard.

Ingredients:
lasagna pasta
sauce (I use store bought, but any sauce will work)
ground meat (I use beef and hot sausage)
mozzarella
ricotta
Italian seasoning (optional)
salt and pepper to taste
other vegetables sliced such as zucchini, tomato, mushrooms

1. Brown and drain meat.
2. Boil pasta to al dente and drain (or skip this by using the "oven ready" pasta).
3. Spread just a little sauce into the pan to keep the pasta from sticking.
4. Mix the mozzarella and ricotta in a bowl. You may wish to add extra seasoning to this mixture.
5. Layer pasta, meat, veggies, cheese, sauce, seasonings. Repeat until the top layer.
6. For the top layer, you want the sauce at the second to last layer and mozzarella as the top layer. Take time to make sure that every bit of exposed pasta is covered by sauce or it will become hard in the oven.
7. Bake at 350. A full 9x13 pan will need about 45-60 minutes. In reality, this could be eaten at any time as the ingredients were precooked, but hot and bubbly lasagna with melted cheese is best!

Mac n cheese

THIS IS ANOTHER CASSEROLE that freezes well. Because the cheese sauce covers all the pasta, it doesn't usually dry out. But, you may want to drizzle with a little cream before baking.

Ingredients:

sasta

milk

mixture of cheeses (at the very least use two like velveeta and mozz, some separate upon melting like cheddar)

ham (optional)

celery & onion (optional)

bread crumbs or crushed Ritz® crackers (optional)

nutmeg

salt and pepper to taste

1. Boil pasta until al dente, drain, and set aside.
2. While the pasta is boiling, cube leftover ham, chop celery and onion. Chop your cheeses into a decent melting size. This is a great time to use up the random blocks of cheese and deli cheese in the fridge. Just be sure to have at least one smooth melting cheese.
3. I use the same pot that I cooked the pasta in to make the sauce. Heat the milk over medium heat and add a dash of nutmeg. Slowly stir in cheese. Add more milk if needed.
4. Once the cheese is melted, stir in ham and/or veggies. Season with parsley, salt and pepper as needed. Remember to taste first, some cheeses are salty, as is ham.
5. Stir in pasta until evenly coated. Pour into 9x13 pan.
6. If desired, sprinkle with extra shredded cheese.
7. If desired, sprinkle with bread crumbs or cracker crumbs.
8. Bake at 350 for 30-45 minutes.

Chicken, Broccoli, Cheddar casserole

I DON'T LIKE FREEZING this casserole as I find the rice dries out more than we like. However, many people do freeze it.

Ingredients:

Rice or riced veggies (riced zucchini shown)
chicken stock
chicken
broccoli
cheddar cheese
milk or cream
1-2 cans of cream of something soup (cream of celery, mushroom, chicken,...)
butter
onion
nutmeg
other seasoning for chicken if desired
salt and pepper to taste
parsley

1. Cook the rice, replacing water with stock for more flavor.
2. Season and cook chicken, then shred or cube. (I usually use leftover chicken so it is already cooked and flavored.)
3. Dice onion and add to chicken part way through cooking.
4. Steam broccoli (or use frozen) and cut into bite size pieces.
5. Mix the ingredients from Steps 1-4 into a 9x13 baking pan. Season with salt and pepper.
6. In the same pot you cooked the rice melt 1-2T of butter. Add cream of something soup and about 1c of milk or cream.
7. Mix in cheddar cheese and stir until melted. Add ¼-½ t nutmeg.
8. Add more cream/milk & seasoning until you have enough to cover the rice mixture in the pan.
9. Sprinkle cheese on top. Bake at 350 for 30-45 minutes (until hot).

Breakfast Casserole

THIS IS A GREAT BREAKFAST to have for a holiday or any other time you want something different. Like most casseroles, it's pretty flexible. I toss in leftover bacon (crumbled) if we only have a piece or two.

Ingredients:
1 pound of breakfast sausage
1 bag of hashbrowns or shred and fry your own potato
6 eggs
1c cream
½ green pepper
½ onion
1c cheddar shredded
salt & pepper

1. Brown the meat and crumble it.
2. Dice and saute the pepper and onion.
3. Layer the hashbrowns on the bottom of the pan.
4. Layer the meat and then the veggies.
5. Whip the eggs, cream, salt and pepper as if you were about to make scrambled eggs.
6. Pour the eggs over the layers in the pan. Sprinkle with the cheddar cheese.
7. Bake at 350 for 45 min or until the egg is completely cooked through.

Beef and Beans

INGREDIENTS:

1 pound of ground beef
2c rice
1 can of baked beans
small amount of onion
salt and pepper to taste

1. Crumble and brown the ground beef. Add diced onion a few minutes before done.
2. Cook the rice (a little softer than you might normally serve is fine).
3. Layer ground beef in a bread pan.
4. Layer rice into the pan.
5. Sprinkle salt and pepper across the rice.
6. Pour baked beans over rice.
7. Bake at 350 until heated through.

Chicken Noodle Casserole

THIS IS ANOTHER GREAT casserole to double batch and freeze one.

1-2 pounds of chicken
3c uncooked pasta
3c shredded cheddar cheese
2c chopped broccoli (fresh or frozen)
1 can of cream of something soup
1T dried Italian seasoning (mix of basil, parsley, oregano)
1c sour cream
½ c milk
salt & pepper to taste
1c crispy fried onions (optional)

1. Dice and cook chicken.
2. Boil and drain pasta.
3. Steam or boil fresh broccoli, frozen needs nothing.
4. Mix together everything except the fried onions which can be used as a topping.
5. Bake at 350 until heated through.

Other meals that don't have a category…

Sheet Pan Dinners

This isn't exactly a casserole, but it's just as easy, maybe easier. I love these in the winter especially. Enjoy your cooking clean up tonight, you only have your serving utensil, pan(s), knife, and maybe bowl and brush from the marinade. Often, when harvesting veggies through the summer and fall I chop them into gallon size bags of mixed veggies just for these dinners. Keep in mind cook times when chopping the vegetables, for example I chop the carrots about ½ the size of the potatoes so they will cook through in the same length of time.

1-2 pounds of meat
meat marinade
1-2 pounds of veggies
vegetable marinade or seasoning

1. Cut and season meat. I usually use chicken or beef and cut it into kebab size chunks or strips.
2. Prepare and season veggies. I like to have a mix of something green like asparagus, and then other rich colors (beets, carrots, etc) and a carb such as potatoes. However, I sometimes just use a "roots" mix (white potato, sweet potato, carrots, beets).
3. Lightly spray the oven and preheat to 375-425.
4. The tricky part of sheet pan dinners is considering the cook times. Beets and carrots tend to take longer to cook than asparagus or beef. Plan accordingly. Begin by laying out an

even layer of the items that cook longest. After they have pre-cooked a few minutes, add a single layer beside them of the next lengthiest cook time item. Continue this process. Use two or three pans if needed to achieve a single layer.

5. About ½ through cook time, flip all items.Season with salt and pepper if needed.

Boiled Ham Dinner

THIS IS ONE OF MY HUSBAND'S favorites. My mother-in-law makes this in a pressure cooker which does a marvelous job of blending the flavors. I use a stock pot on the stove or a crock pot.

Ingredients:
ham
potatoes
carrots
turnip
cabbage
stock or water
salt and pepper to taste
serve with mustard

1. Peel and chop vegetables to an even cooking time size. In other words, I cut the potatoes larger and the carrots smaller so they need to cook for an equal time.
2. We don't actually like to eat the onion, turnip, or the cabbage, but find their taste is required to round out the dish. Therefore, I tend to leave these in large chunks to make them easy to avoid, but so they infuse their flavor into the dish. If you like them, chop them smaller to be sure that they cook evenly with the other vegetables.
3. Place the ham in the center of the pot and pour the vegetables around it. Season it all with salt and pepper (go easy on the salt as some ham is crazy-salty).
4. Cover with liquid, either water or stock. Bring to a boil and then return to simmer for hours. The cook time will be dependent upon the size of the ham and how many vegetables you use. Typically I put ours on around noon to eat around 5...

Some prefer to fork-mash the vegetables upon their plate and drizzle with some broth then mustard. I like my veggies bite sized. As long as everyone eats, does it matter?

Sweet Potato Boats

WE LIKE THESE "UNSTUFFED" as much as stuffed, maybe more. In other words we like it with all the sweet potato flesh scooped out rather than served in the skin.

Ingredients:
1# ground pork
2 sweet potatoes
4 bunches onion/scallions
½ t ginger
¼ c broth
sour cream
monterey jack cheese
cumin, garlic powder, paprika to taste
salt and pepper to taste

1. Brown ground pork, remove any extra grease.
2. Poke the skins with a fork and then microwave sweet potatoes until soft - about 6-10 minutes.
3. Chop scallions in small pieces. Stir in the pork. Add oil if needed to keep from sticking to the pan (the level of fat in pork varies a great deal whether there is too much or not enough).
4. Add ginger, then other spices and stir to coat meat.
5. After about a minute add broth (I use chicken).
6. Halve and then scoop flesh out of sweet potatoes to form "boats" (the potato halves are hollowed out to form a canoe shape). Add this scooped out flesh to the pork mixture and stir in.
7. Cook down until the liquid evaporates.
8. Spoon pork mixture into boats (over rice or just onto a plate) and garnish with sour cream and cheese as desired.

Zucchini Boats

THESE HAVE SO MANY different flavor possibilities. It's fantastic in the middle of zucchini season.

Ingredients:
young to medium zucchini (or summer squash)
sauce
cheese
fillings

1. Cut off the blossom and stem ends of the zucchini if they look tough, cut as little as possible.
2. Slice the zucchini in ½ lengthwise. Scoop out the seeds and some of the flesh leaving a canoe shaped zucchini.
3. Some people salt and pepper their boats, I never bother to.
4. In a separate bowl, you want to mix your filling (see ideas below), then spoon into boats.
5. If the filling is dry you may want to drizzle on some more sauce.
6. Sprinkle with cheese.
7. Bake on slightly greased pan for about 20-30 minutes at 400. You may want to broil for a minute or two to fully melt the cheese.

Filling ideas:

- Use cooked rice to bulk up any filling

- Bar-b-q theme, use pulled pork or shredded chicken with bbq sauce

- Pizza theme, use pizza toppings and pizza sauce

- Summer Italian theme, shred summer veggies, sprinkle with Italian seasonings like basil, parsley, oregano, and a marinara sauce

- Ground pork as described for the Stuffed Sweet Potatoes above.

- Taco theme, use browned beef, taco seasoning (I use the packets of seasoning), cooked rice, salsa, and cheese. (I've seen it topped with lettuce and tomato after cooking, but we don't do this.)

- Leftovers, use whatever you think will work. Make sure there's a sauce and cheese makes everything better (except dessert).

Baked goods

Muffins

Almost any bread recipe can be turned into muffins or rolls. Quick breads (no rising time) are best for muffins. This recipe is so versatile you can switch out the flavors in a variety of ways. You may need to adjust the moisture a tad, just adjust the amount of milk.

Ingredients:

1 1/2c flour

½ c oatmeal

1c sugar

1c chopped fruit, chocolate chips, nuts, or whatever filling you want.

½ c butter or a little less (more often in the summer I find I need to use a little less or the muffins feel greasy on the bottom)

2 eggs

1/2c+ milk

2t baking powder

1t vanilla

a dash of spice as you like (nutmeg, cinnamon, ginger,...)

This muffin recipe is sweet, almost cake like, but dense and filling. Switching out the oatmeal for flour will make it a little lighter, but I liked the health benefit of the oatmeal.

1. Lightly mix all the dry ingredients together.
2. Blend in butter.
3. Create a well in the center and add liquid ingredients. Lightly

mix. (begin with only 1/2c of milk. Addmore if needed after mixing in the filling.)

4. Lastly add the 1c of filling.
5. Spoon into greased or paper muffin cups about ⅔ full. The mixture should be just a little thicker than pudding.
6. Bake at 350 for about 20 minutes. (325 for mini muffins for about 12-15 minutes.)

Banana Bread

BANANAS ARE ONE OF those fruits that I buy most often. Luckily I like them greenish yellow while my son likes them about a day yellower. But still, no one likes them once they have spots or begin to turn brown. After a day or so, (because it's just not a high priority) I peel them and put 2-3 in a sandwich bag and freeze them. They will turn brown, usually, in the freezer, but they taste just fine. They also release a fair amount of liquid as they thaw, but use that too. Sometimes we use these for smoothies, but most often for baking.

This is a great recipe to make with toddlers as it's super easy and they love to snack on what they made.

Ingredients:

2-3 bananas

1 1/2c flour

½ c oatmeal (you can use just flour but oatmeal makes it more moist)

1c sugar

1/2c butter

2 eggs

baking soda

1-2 t vanilla

dash of cinnamon

1. Lightly mix all of the ingredients together. I often use a glass bowl so I can warm up the butter and the frozen bananas for 15-30 seconds. Do not worry about it being perfectly smooth, but try to get all the flour incorporated.
2. Pour into a lightly greased bread pan.
3. Bake at 350 for about 45-55 minutes, until the top is cracked and the loaf has a hollow sound when tapped.

Beer bread

THIS IS SUPER EASY bread to bake. The alcohol cooks out so you just have the taste of the beer. We often serve this with soups or stews. I also sell a lot of these loaves and people love sandwiches made with it.

Ingredients:

3c flour

1/3c brown sugar

4 1/2t baking powder

dash of salt

1 bottle or can (12 oz) of beer. The flavors of the beer will affect the taste of your bread.

1. Mix all dry ingredients.
2. Pour in the beer, allow the foam to subside a little.
3. Mix until just blended.
4. Pour into a lightly greased loaf pan.
5. Bake 45-60 minutes at 350* (I usually bake it for about 50 minutes, but weather, especially humidity affects this) the bread cracks on top and sounds a bit hollow when done.

Carrot Raisin Bread

I FOUND THIS RECIPE when I needed to use up some carrots. Now I keep shredded carrots in the freezer just for this.

Ingredients:

2c shredded Carrots

2c flour

1c raisins (soaked in water)

1c milk

1/4c oil

1/4c sugar

2t baking powder

1t cinnamon

1/2t baking soda

1/2t salt

1/4t nutmeg

If you use a plant based milk this is an excellent vegan recipe, and handy therefore for potlucks or family dinners.

1. Soak the raisins in warm water for 30+ minutes to soften them. Drain water.
2. Combine all ingredients in a bowl until just mixed.
3. Pour into a greased loaf pan or muffin tins.
4. Bake at 400 for about 45 minutes/loaf or 18-20 minutes/ muffins.

Cook ahead and portion for microwave meals

I bring my lunch to work everyday. It's funny, at home for lunch I'm completely content to have sandwiches, but when I go to work, I want to eat something warm and savory for lunch. A sandwich just doesn't cut it. Sometimes I have leftovers that I can take, but more often I need something that I can just grab and go from the freezer.

A previous chapter covered casseroles, and admittedly I am a fan of bringing mac and cheese for lunch. When I'm prepping these, I often mix in some ground beef for a little protein, staying-power. Sometimes, I add in some cajun seasoning or something different for variety. Soups work well too, but be forewarned that cream often separates when frozen so it won't look as nice, although the taste is still good.

Admittedly, I often spend a day making up 3-5 portions of each of these, so very seldom are they fully from scratch.

Veggie noodles with meat sauce

THIS SUMMER I HOPE to "zoodle" a bunch of vegetables and freeze them to be ready to make this dish. I do have the little gadget to do it, but right now I'm actually willing to pay for the premade veggie spirals that look like noodles. My local store carries the "zoodles" from both a yellow squash and zucchini. I use both for the greater vitamins and color. I cook all of this in one pot, but I set the noodles and ground meat aside after cooking.

Ingredients:

2-3 packages of veggie noodles.

1 pound or more of ground beef or your choice of meat(s)
as many veggies chopped or shredded as you like
tomato sauce
Italian seasoning
oil
salt and pepper (to taste)
cheese (optional)
hot pepper flakes (optional)

Directions:

Quickly saute the veggie noodles and drain the excess liquid. Set aside.

Brown one pound of ground beef or meat of your choice. You do need a protein to keep that full feeling longer. Season as you like, I use a little salt and pepper.

Saute or cook your vegetables through until they are tender. For example, I start with a little oil and my onion first, then peppers, followed by shredded carrots... Season to taste, I use a lot of Italian Seasoning and a little pepper.

Add your tomato sauce to the veggies. In a well prepared year I would have my own canned tomato sauce, most of the time I use store bought sauce. Stir in your cooked meat. Simmer to meld the flavors. Adjust seasoning as necessary.

Add the veggie noodles and cook until those noodles are hot.

Turn off, but leave on the hot burner and let cool. This allows for the flavors to further mix with each other. Also, portioning the food when it is cool is easier. This step can be skipped, but I usually am prepping several meals at once, so it works for me.

Finally, add cheese and/or hot pepper flakes if you like.

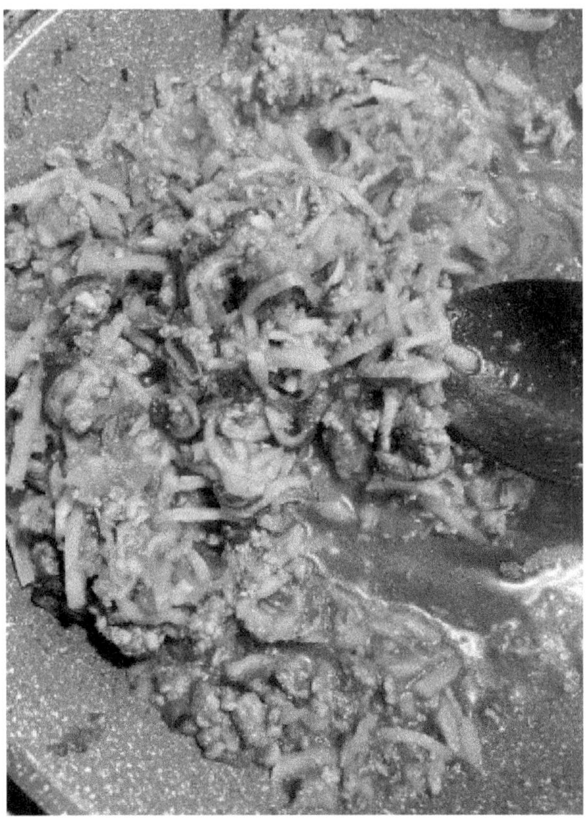

Spinach & Tortellini soup

THIS IS THE EASIEST soup that I make, because it's almost entirely prepackaged ingredients that I then tweak. Because of all the prepackaged pieces, I think the sodium may be pretty high; I would not add any salt to this recipe.

Ingredients:

1 large can of Italian seasoned diced tomatoes.
chicken stock (I vary how much)
1 package of frozen spinach
1 package of frozen tortellini (I use the tricolor cheese tortellini)
cream

1 small onion

butter

random other leftovers that can be added

Italian Seasoning

pepper

Directions:

Peel, dice, and saute the onion until transparent

Add the can of tomatoes and the chicken stock. Add more stock than you think you will need because the tortellini will absorb some.

Stir in the spinach and simmer until warm.

Taste and adjust your seasoning. I almost always add more of the Italian seasoning as there isn't enough in the canned tomatoes.

Add the tortellini and any other random leftovers that seem to fit.

Simmer and taste test.

Near the end of cooking add cream in a ratio of about 1:2 of cream to stock.

Serving this immediately when hot is delicious, especially with thick bread. However, it works well to freeze and reheat. The cream does not usually separate when freezing.

Stir Fry

HERE'S ANOTHER THAT I cheat on, but I also use up leftovers in.

Ingredients:

½ of one large frozen Teriyaki Stir Fry kit (the ones with the shredded veggies, short noodles, and pouches of teriyaki sauce)

½-1 pound of chicken or pork, cubed (you could use beef too, but maybe adjust your seasoning some...)

any additional vegetables you want to add

oil

salt n pepper as needed.

Directions:

Begin by sauteing the meat if it hasn't already been cooked.

Add in any vegetables that you have on hand that haven't been cooked.

Once the meat is cooked through and the vegetables are tender, stir in the stir fry mix (no sauce yet) and simmer with a little water to prevent sticking.

Once the mix has completely thawed, pour in ½ the seasoning pouch.

Stir, cook through, and add seasoning if desired.

These are not gourmet meals, but they sure beat sandwiches and the more veggies you add, the healthier they are!

Carrot ginger soup

THIS SOUP TASTES GREAT despite the fact that it looks like baby food! I use this recipe as my base, but I change around the seasoning depending upon my mood.

INGREDIENTS:

- 1-2 pounds of carrots peeled and chopped into large pieces
- ½ an onion chopped
- 2-4 celery stalks chopped
- 2 c broth (I use chicken broth)
- 2 c cream
- 4 T butter
- 1 ½ t ginger
- 1 ½ t cumin

(dash of celery seeds if you didn't use celery stalks)
1t paprika
Salt and pepper to taste

1. This is a soup that can be made quickly but I prefer to simmer everything but the cream over a long period of time so the flavors merge better.
2. Once the carrots are soft, blend the ingredients together.
3. Add the cream and blend again.
4. Taste and adjust your seasonings.

Seafood

We tend to buy lobster when it is cheapest (softshell) and often boil/steam it and freeze to use later for chowders and rolls. Only the stuffed lobster recipe below needs fresh lobster.

Stuffed Lobster

THIS IS A MEAL THAT my husband makes, largely because he's the one who likes it the most. Personally, I like to do this with soft-shell lobsters, 1, because they are cheaper, but two, their shells are easier to crack.

Ingredients:
3 small lobster (or one large and one small)
a sleeve or two of buttery crackers (we use Ritz ®)
4-6 oz butter
garlic
Italian seasoning (oregano, parsley, basil)
salt and pepper to taste
optional: diced onion and celery

1. Begin by stabbing the knife into the head and cracking open two of the lobsters along their back and down their tail. Do this as quickly as possible to kill them cleanly. The third lobster (or the small one if you just split the large one) should be head stabbed to kill it as quickly as possible and then broken however you like to remove the meat from the claws and tail.

1. Chop up the meat from the last small lobster into small pieces, this will be for the stuffing.
2. Melt the butter
3. Crush the crackers into fine pieces then mix with most of the melted butter.
4. Season the stuffing (crackers & butter) with garlic, Italian seasoning, salt and pepper to taste.
5. Some people like to finely chop celery and onion for the stuffing, or add a little dried onion flakes.
6. Add the chopped lobster to the stuffing and mix well.
7. Evenly spread the stuffing into the open lobster(s).
8. Bake at 400 for about 10 minutes (this depends on the size of your lobster to cook it through) and then broil 1-2 minutes to make the stuffing crispy.
9. Enjoy! The leftover butter is for dipping the claw meat into.

Seafood Bisque

WE ALWAYS ASSUMED THIS was difficult based on restaurant prices. It's not.

Ingredients:

2-3c seafood of your choice. (We use cooked lobster and shrimp)

2-3c broth (I use chicken)

1c cream

2-3T butter

flour (optional)

1t dried onion flakes

Old Bay Seasoning to taste

paprika

salt and a little pepper to taste

parsley (optional)

The cream is the very last thing that you add so that it doesn't separate. Keep it in the fridge until about 20 minutes before serving.

1. Chop seafood into bite-size pieces.
2. Roux (optional) - whisk about 1T of flour into 2Tbutter. As your paste forms but before it burns slowly whisk in 1T broth. Keep slowly adding flour & butter to keep growing the paste. Add broth as needed to keep it from scorching. Then slowly add broth to create a creamy textured broth.
3. Combine seafood, broth, onion flakes, (butter if you didn't make a roux), Old Bay seasoning and salt. If you are combining raw seafood, do not taste to season until the seafood is fully cooked.
4. Simmer for 30 minutes to two hours. Taste for seasoning.
5. About 20 minutes before serving stir in cream. Heat to serve.
6. Garnish with parsley and serve with warm bread.

Bacon wrapped scallops

THIS ONE IS SUPER YUMMY, but we don't do it often.

Ingredients:
scallops
bacon
butter
maple syrup
salt
toothpicks

1. I normally bake my bacon on baking sheets, sometimes I broil it (depending on the levels of distraction), but for this I cut the strips of bacon in half and partially cook the bacon in a pan. You want the bacon half cooked rather than burn the scallops.
2. For the ease of cleanup, I tend to cover a baking sheet with tinfoil, but you could just lightly grease the pan.
3. Wrap each scallop with a piece of bacon and secure with a toothpick.
4. After all the scallops are wrapped, melt the butter then mix in maple syrup and salt to taste. I tend to use very little salt, more can always be added later depending on the salt level of the bacon.
5. Lightly drizzle the scallops with the butter syrup mixture.
6. Bake for about 10 minutes at 400. Remove and flip the scallops.
7. Lightly drizzle with the butter and syrup mixture. Depending on the size of your scallops, bake another 4-7 minutes.
8. Serve with the butter mixture as a garnish.

Too Many Eggs!

Every once in a while we don't use as many eggs or I don't sell as many eggs as I expect and we have an overabundance of them. These are some of our favorite ways to use up the extra.

French Toast Sticks

THIS WORKS BEST WITH older (not quite stale) bread or a bread that is looser/more airy. You want the egg mixture to soak in, but you also need it to completely cook. I always burn my fingers a little doing this so I recommend you let the sticks cool ever so slightly before rolling them in the cinnamon and sugar.

Ingredients:
loaf of bread
18+ eggs
½-1c milk
¼-1/2t of nutmeg
½ t cinnamon
1T vanilla
Cinnamon and sugar to taste

1. Heat your pan to med high, spray or melt butter.
2. Begin by slicing the bread into sticks. I do this by stacking about four pieces of bread on top of each other and quartering them into sticks.
3. When about ½ the loaf is sliced, create your egg mixture.
4. Whisk all the eggs, with as much milk as you think looks

right. Mix in vanilla, cinnamon, and nutmeg. You'll have to re-stir this occasionally.

5. When the pan is hot, press some sticks into the egg mixture to completely coat them and to soak in a little (again it depends on the thickness and density of the bread but you must be able to cook the egg all the way through without burning the bread).
6. Cook the sticks in the pan leaving space so that you can easily flip them.
7. On a plate or in a pie dish mix cinnamon and sugar to roll the sticks in.
8. When the sticks are golden and cooked through, remove them from the pan, and drop in sugar mixture. Place the next batch of egg soaked sticks into the pan.
9. Roll the cooked sticks in the butter and then remove to another plate to cool.
10. Repeat.

By coating them in sugar and cinnamon you eliminate the need for syrup making these a great snack to freeze in batches and then microwave as needed, ready to grab and go. Eating them immediately is also yummy!

Quiche

I'M TERRIBLE AT MAKING pie crust, it's either light and flakey or dense and thick. So I cheat and buy premade dough a lot of the time. This also works well with a cracker crumb crust. This recipe is just a general idea as you can use almost any veggies or cooked meats or cheeses in this. These do freeze ok for a couple weeks (precooked), the crust may get funky if you freeze for more than a month.

Ingredients
1 pie crust per quiche
6-10 eggs
⅓ c milk
1c+veggies chopped to bitesize
1c+ meat crumbled or shredded to bite size
1/2c+ shredded cheese
salt and pepper

1. Lay out the crust in your pie dish. Some people swear by taking a fork and poking the bottom a few times to prevent any bubbling. I've never had an issue with this.
2. Preheat the oven to 400*.
3. Chop your veggies, then crumble or shred your meats.
4. Whisk your eggs, milk, salt and pepper in a bowl and then pour into the crust.
5. Spread the veggies and/or meats through the egg mixture in your pie. You want these spread evenly, use your fingers not a fork so you do not damage the pie crust.
6. Sprinkle cheese across the top.
7. Depending on how thick your pie is, bake for about 15 minutes at 400, then turn down to 375 for another 20+ minutes. I would rather cook too long and have a darker crust than risk having my eggs undercooked, but use your best

judgment.

8. Serve immediately, or freeze and then reheat in the oven.

Animal feed

WHEN IN DOUBT OR A state of overwhelm: Scramble and cook the eggs (no seasoning or milk needed) then feed to your animals.

Dogs will love them, but have nasty farts. You may want to scramble and freeze in portions for your indoor pets. Outdoor animals will love the extra protein too.

Desserts

Magic bars

Ingredients

2 c graham cracker crumbs

1/2 c (1 stick) melted butter

14 oz (1 can) sweetened condensed milk

1 c semi-sweet chocolate chips

1 c shredded sweetened coconut

This recipe is super simple and some of us love it. There is a member of the family who doesn't like coconut, they're just out of luck. The best part of this recipe is that you can add and swap out ingredients pretty easily. Want butterscotch instead of chocolate chips? No problem! Want to add nuts? No problem!

1. Crush the graham crackers. I use a gallon size bag and put a few crackers in at a time, then roll and crush with a rolling pin or glass. You want the crumbs pretty fine. Save the bag to store the bars in.
2. Simultaneously to crushing graham crackers, melt the butter in a bowl. Combine cracker crumbs and butter.
3. Make sure all the crumbs are coated with butter so that they stick together when pressed. Spread and press down as a crust in your 9x13 pan. Some people just grease the pan, I lay parchment paper in it to make the clean up easier.
4. Pour and spread the sweetened condensed milk over the crust.

5. Spread your ingredients in layers. Leave the coconut until last so it will toast in the oven.
6. Bake at 350 for about 30 minutes, until the edges pull away slightly from the sides.
7. Cool completely before cutting. If you used parchment paper you will be able to cool, lift out the paper, and easily cut.
8. You may want to store these in the fridge to avoid any melting in warm weather. While delicious they can be a gooey mess.

Crescent Rolls® w/apple

THIS IS POTENTIALLY the easiest dessert or appetizer ever.

Ingredients:
Crescent Rolls®
apples
cinnamon and sugar to taste

1. Peel and slice the apples. The thicker you slice the apples the firmer they will be, the thinner the slices the softer they will be.
2. Coat apples by tossing in a cinnamon & sugar mixture.
3. Roll the apple slices into the rolls. Depending on the size of your apples you may choose to cut the dough triangles in half (smaller triangles).
4. Sprinkle the rolls with the cinnamon and sugar mixture if desired.
5. Bake as directed on the package.
6. Serve plain or with vanilla ice cream.

Strawberry Shortcake

THIS CAN BE MADE WITH any berries, but strawberries are our favorite.

Ingredients:
2 c berries (sliced if large)
biscuits
2-3c heavy whipping cream
sugar to taste
1t vanilla

I often cheat with this recipe, depending on my time and energy level. I'm not opposed to making it with those butter flavored biscuits that come in a can and with store bought whip cream. You might also substitute ice cream for the whipped cream.

1. Slice berries if they are large like strawberries, and dust with sugar. If you let them sit for a few hours the juices will start to pool out.
2. Bake your biscuits.
3. Whip your cream until soft peaks form. Add vanilla and gently fold in sugar. Do not overwork.*
4. Serve with berries scooped over halved biscuits and topped with whipped cream.

*If you overwork or overbeat your cream one of two things will happen. You may form butter, or the cream will break and you will be left with sticky liquid. Beat or whip the cream (I use an electric mixer) until soft peaks form. "Soft peaks" means when you lift the beater or whisk out of the cream it pulls the cream up into a mountain peak form. If untouched, that peak slowly sinks to a rounded shape instead of a jagged mountain top.

Cookies

THIS IS ONE OF MY FAVORITE chapters!

One of the greatest tips I have about baking cookies is to broil them. No, I kid you not! I like my cookies firm, but soft and chewy. So sometime as a kid I realized that by the time I had the top a nice golden color either my cookies were crunchy or maybe even scorched on the bottom. So I started experimenting. I soon found that I could bake them for about ¾ of the time and then broil them for about a minute (watch this closely!!). This has a short window of success, but leads to amazing cookies. As an adult, I also learned that other things come into play like the type of flour and whether your eggs and butter are cold or warm, but I always split my blazing into baking and broiling.

My other tip is to use parchment paper when baking. I began doing this when we learned that my son had food allergies, some of which could be triggered by baking sprays or even possibly oils left on the pan from a prior dish. We didn't know if he had any tolerance to even a microscopic amount of "contamination" ie. nut or sesame oil.

I can usually bake an entire batch of cookies on 2-3 sheets, rotating them through cooling and reloading so I only need three sheets of paper. Most of the time I can save those and use them a second time, before the paper gets used for firestarter. I felt bad creating waste with disposable pan lining, but his health comes first. Moreover, it was a really handy way to slide the cookies off the pan and separate layers for storage (if I didn't save the paper for the next round of baking).

Chocolate Chip Cookies

(MY FAVORITE BY THE way)

Ingredients:

2 sticks of butter (softened)

2 c flour

2 eggs

½ c white sugar

½ c brown sugar

1-3 t vanilla

1/2t baking soda

Chocolate chips or chunks to taste (1- 1 ½ c)

Directions:

Cream together the butter, sugars, and vanilla. Add in the eggs, flour, and baking soda. Once it is well mixed, pour in the chocolate chips and mix just enough to evenly distribute the chocolate (but not so long it breaks down the chocolate chips. You can add chocolate powder at this stage, too.)

Clean batter and chill for at least fifteen minutes while preheating the oven to 375*.

Spread cookies on the baking sheet (I use parchment paper but you can used a greased cookie sheet). Allow room for the cookies to spread some. The colder your butter was and the longer you chill your dough the less spreading there will be.

I spread my cookies in a row of 3 then 2 then 3 then 2,...depends on the size of the pan.

Bake for 5 minutes, then broil on high for 1 minute. You may need to bake or broil longer, usually I find 6-7 minutes baking and 1.5 minutes broiling is good, but it depends on the weather and temperature inside my kitchen. Watch the cookies carefully when broiling!

Allow to cool on a rack until firm (again parchment paper is hand as it will keep the melted chocolate from dripping down).

Store in an airtight container.

Lemon Crinkle Cookies

I DON'T USE EITHER of the optional ingredients, but many people do.

Ingredients:

1 stick of butter

1 c sugar

2 eggs

2 1/4c flour

2T lemon juice

2 t baking powder

Confectioners sugar (optional)

Yellow food coloring (optional)

Directions:

Cream together the butter, sugar, and lemon juice, then the two eggs.

Then slowly add the flour and baking powder.

Add food coloring if desired.

Once completely mixed chill for at least 15 minutes while preheating the oven to 350*.

Roll into balls about the size of a golf ball. Flatten with a fork.

Dip in confectioner's sugar if desired.

Bak about 9-10 minutes and then broil on high about 1 minute. Bake longer if needed.

Cool on baking sheets and store in an airtight container.

Gingersnaps

INGREDIENTS:

1 ½ sticks of butter

2 1/4c flour

2 eggs

½ c white sugar

½ c molasses

2 t baking soda

1T vinegar

1 t cinnamon

1 t ginger

1/2 t cloves

Directions:

Cream together the butter, sugar, molasses, and spices.

Add in the eggs and then the dry ingredients. Finally add in the vinegar.

Chill for at least 15 minutes while preheating the oven to 325*.

Roll into golf-ball sized balls, dip in sugar if desired, then flatten with a fork on the baking sheet.

Bake for about 10 minutes, but check after 6 minutes. Broil about 1 minute.

Cool on baking racks then store in an airtight container.

Dehydrator

I love using my dehydrator just as much as canning because it saves space in my freezer. It's pretty easy too, after the initial prep work you set it and forget about it for hours at a time.

Apple jerky

I FIRST STARTED MAKING this when I was in danger of losing the last of the apples we had picked. I couldn't make applesauce fast enough. I tend to usually make this in sliced form, but I also dice them much finer to use in oatmeal, too.

While I use a dehydrator, these can be made in the oven, either on baking racks over baking sheets (to catch drippings) or directly on the sheets and turned periodically. Do not spray the sheets with any oil.

1. Peel and slice the apples as evenly as possible. The smaller or thinner the pieces, then the quicker they will dry. Keeping the pieces to the same size and thickness helps them to dry evenly at the same rate.

1. In a bowl, add the slices and cinnamon sugar to taste. This will vary dependent upon how you prefer the flavors and how tart the apples are. Remember that the cinnamon and sugar will become more pronounced as the apples dry.

1. The weather, the machine's temperature, the thickness of the fruit, and how closely together they are spaced all affect the

drying times. After a few hours of drying check it and keep monitoring the progress. I usually have to switch myu trays around at least once. The apples will still be soft and bendable when dry but warm. If you are not sure if they are dry enough, you can let them cool and then test, then dry more or store.

Store in an airtight container, in a cool, dry, and dark (like a cupboard) location. Eat these plain, or add to oatmeal before adding the boiling water.

Fruit roll ups

THESE WERE AWESOME when my children were younger. Often it was a three part process as they would help me pick the apples. Then I made applesauce (can be canned or frozen), and then some of that applesauce was used for fruit roll ups.

These may not have a huge nutritional value, but they are good tasting and cheaper than what we purchased. The sugar content was a bit better, too. We started out making the healthy ones that were just fruit purees - applesauce was the regular base and then we added peach or strawberry, or...However, the kids didn't really like the fruit leathers. So I started doing them this way.

Ingredients:
about 1 quart of applesauce
1 box of jello ® mix
parchment or wax paper

1. Mix well.
2. Lightly spray your drying trays with a bland oil (coconut oil is actually tasty for this) OR cut parchment paper to size. I always used the spray and let cool completely before attempting to remove the fruit. I had a few stick...
3. Pour and spread into trays. This should be about ¼" thick, but you may need to adjust based upon your machine. Too thin and it will tear when you try to remove, or will dry with holes. Too thick and it will take a very long time to dry.
4. After a few hours, check for dryness. Continue to check regularly. If you are unsure, allow to cool completely and then check. I usually have a few trays that are poured in thicker and take longer. I struggle with pouring evenly.
5. Carefully and slowly peel off of trays. You may find it helpful to cut (I use a plastic knife to avoid scratching my trays) into

serving sizes and peel smaller sections instead of trying to remove the whole sheet.

6. Place servings onto wax paper or parchment paper cut to little larger than the fruit roll up.
7. Roll up. Store in an airtight container in the fridge.

These can last a few days out on the counter in an airtight container, but they will mold fairly quickly at room temperature. To be safe, I always refrigerate. I know they last at least two weeks in our fridge, but we've never had any left after that. I would expect (but not guarantee) that in an airtight container in the fridge, that they could last a long time.

Green Powder (veggie powder)

YOU CAN EITHER USE this powder to sprinkle into anything you want to have more vitamins, or you can make your own vitamin capsules. It really depends on your health, your needs, and your wants. I am not a nutritionist so I would never attempt to tell you what ratios to use to make your own vitamins, but it wouldn't be that hard to research and do.

You can do this one of two ways: Either buy extra veggies to do this with, or use up some excess from your garden before it goes to waste. Alternatively, use those little leftovers of a spoonful of peas here and two spoonfuls of corn there...if you don't have chickens or animals to feed these to, consider having a container in the freezer and spoon the veggies into. Then dehydrate when you have enough. Waste not, want not?

If possible you want to chop, dice, or slice your veggies very evenly by type to make the drying times easier. In other words, if you are drying tomatoes, have all the tomato slices pretty even. If you are drying celery, chop the celery evenly. You absolutely want these veggies to be completely dry.

Blanche the chopped, sliced, or diced veggies for about a minute. Drain.

Spread evenly on the trays without the pieces touching.

Dry until crispy or brittle. You may need to cool and test them several times as vegetables may still be pliant (bendy) when warm.

You can store in an airtight container and use in soups and stews just as they are, but allow time for these vegetables to absorb water and soften.

Or, store in an airtight container until you are ready to grind them.

I use a coffee grinder, you can also use a spice grinder. I usually mix my veggies together, but you could certainly have separate jars of red pepper, celery, kale,...

The vegetables you choose to use will determine how strong of a taste this powder has. You can add quite a lot to sauces, soups, and casseroles without anyone knowing. You can add some to smoothies and juice before the taste is noticeable. Brownies also hide the taste quite well.

Preserves & pickles

Dilly carrots

I'm not a huge fan of dill, but my family is. Lots of people make dilly beans, but I had these for a side once in some little sandwich shop and the bright pop of dilly carrots are amazing. These also sell great at farmers markets!

I tend to slice all that I need for the pickles, then I take my leftover "ugly" pieces and chop up the extra carrot chunks for blanching and freezing. I make up bags of these beets, carrots, potatoes, sweet potatoes etc to quick-bake as a side.

Ingredients:

2 pounds carrots
1 cup white vinegar
1 cup water
1 tablespoon pickling salt
1 teaspoon dill seed
1/2 teaspoon pepper
2 tablespoons minced garlic
hot pepper flakes to taste

1. Peel carrots
2. Cut to length for the jars (about ⅛" below rim), then slice lengthwise.
3. Fill jars leaving about ⅛" headspace (space between the beets and where the lid will rest).

4. In a separate pot, heat water, vinegar, garlic, and spices to boil.
5. Pour liquid over carrots in jars.
6. Wipe clean jars and finger tighten lids to jars.
7. Boil water in your water canner. Process jars based on your elevation and size of jars.

Pickled beets

I LOVE BEETS STEAMED and baked, but pickled gives a sweet tart side garnish. I tend to slice all that I need for the pickles, then I take my leftover "ugly" slices and chop up the extra beets for blanching and freezing. I make up bags of these beets, carrots, potatoes, sweet potatoes etc to quick-bake as a side.

Ingredients:

10 pounds beets
2 cups white sugar
1 tablespoon pickling salt
1 quart white vinegar
¼ cup whole cloves or to taste
Some people add slices of onion, but I do not

1. Peel the beets. Some people blanch them for a moment and then the peels are softer. I usually just peel them raw.
2. Slice the beets at about ⅛-¼" Just be uniform with whatever thickness you choose.
3. Fill the jars, leaving about ½" headspace (space between the beets and where the lid will rest).
4. In a separate pot, heat vinegar, sugar, and spices to boil.
5. Pour liquid over beets in jars.
6. Wipe clean jars and finger tighten lids to jars.
7. Boil water in your water canner. Process jars based on your elevation and size of jars.

Zucchini relish

THIS IS A GREAT WAY to use up zucchini when they get too big (that takes like a day!) or you just have too many!

Ingredients:

2 pounds cucumbers
1 1/2 cups white vinegar
1/4 cup sugar
4 teaspoons pickling salt
1 teaspoon mustard seeds
1 teaspoon coriander seeds
3/4 teaspoon dill seeds
2 cups water
3/4 cup coarsely chopped dill
3 garlic cloves, minced

1. Shred the zucchini by hand or better yet with some sort of food processor.
2. Fill jars leaving about ¼" headspace (space between the beets and where the lid will rest).
3. In a separate pot, heat vinegar, sugar, and spices to boil.
4. Pour liquid into jars.
5. Wipe clean jars and finger tighten lids to jars.
6. Boil water in your water canner. Process jars based on your elevation and size of jars.

Fruit butters

FRUIT BUTTERS ARE A nice alternative to the very sweet jellies and jams while still adding a touch of sweet to your toast or muffin. Apple Butter is the best known fruit butter, but try others - plum has an almost chocolate taste. While not a fruit, I particularly like pumpkin as well, it's like pumpkin pie on your toast.

You can cook this on the stovetop but I find it easiest in the crockpot. I actually cook my fruit or pumpkin in the crockpot and then puree it in the blender. Then I return it to the crockpot and add sugar and spices.

Ingredients:

2-3c fruit puree (ie. applesauce)

sugar

spices (cinnamon is most common, also nutmeg)

Wash and peel your fruit as needed, and cook until soft, then puree.

Add the sugar and spices. Add a little less than what you think you need as the flavors will strengthen as it cooks down.

Cook the fruit puree until it is thicker than applesauce.

Taste and season as the puree reaches the desired thickness.

Spoon the fruit butter into jars.

Wipe clean jars and finger tighten lids to jars.

Boil water in your water canner. Process jars based on your elevation and size of jars.

Flavored salts

Flavored salts are awesome and can be used on salads, meats, or even mixed drinks. Salt often enhances a food's natural flavors but a flavored salt adds just a little accent of another flavor. But do not season too heavily, the flavors are strong. Use a good salt, like sea salt or kosher salt. I like the large grains as it is easier to see how much has been used, and it is pretty.

Pickle salt

THIS IS REALLY GREAT on popcorn!

Ingredients:

fresh dill weed chopped fine or the dill pickle (or bread and butter) seasoning packets

Salt

Directions:

1. In a large bowl mix the pickle favoring and the salt together until mixed evenly
2. Dehydrate or bake on very low temp until the dill is completely dry.
3. Periodically stir and respread to help the drying process.

Your goal is to completely dry this to make it shelf-stable. Any moisture can make the flavored salt mold.

Wine Salt

THIS IS GREAT ON MEATS, especially.

Ingredients:

leftover red wine (you know that ½ glass or so that is about to resemble vinegar? lol)

salt

Directions:

Pour the wine into a pot and begin to reduce.

When the wine has reduced by about ½ stir in salt, about a 1:1 ratio. Continue reducing at a low temperature until most of the liquid has evaporated. This happens quickly.

Spread out evenly on a baking sheet and bake at a low temperature. You can also use a dehydrator. Periodically stir and respread to help the drying process.

Your goal is to completely dry this to make it shelf-stable. Any moisture can make the flavored salt mold.

Herbed Salt

THIS CAN BE DONE WITH any combination of herbs you want and therefore can be used on any meat or fish, on freshly baked bread, on popcorn,...

Ingredients:

fresh herb chopped fine or dry herbs crushed

salt

Directions:

1. In a large bowl mix the herbs and the salt together until mixed evenly
2. Dehydrate or bake on very low temp until the dill is

completely dry.

3. Periodically stir and respread to help the drying process.

Your goal is to completely dry this to make it shelf-stable. Any moisture can make the flavored salt mold.

Waste Not Want Not

Sometimes I do really well in this category, but often I have to decide between the value of my time and the worth of the leftovers. The chickens win as often as I do. Still, I try to find good uses for the little bits of leftovers if they don't actually work together for being put together as a brown-bag lunch meal.

Old bread?

I'M ALWAYS TEMPTED to try making bread pudding, but here's the thing. I don't think I would actually like it.

Occasionally, I buy too much bread thinking that we'll be eating a lot of sandwiches, and then we don't. So before the bread goes stale, I often turn it into french toast or french toast sticks (these seem to freeze and reheat better).

But more often than not, what's leftover are the two heels of the loaf and maybe the second to last slice.

My mother used to make stuffing from bread about to be stale. Also, I could easily make croutons (another thing I don't like) but usually I make breadcrumbs because that is what we use the most. Old crackers can also be added to this.

I make breadcrumbs because we use them the most, but also because it is super easy. You can mix together a whole bunch of different kinds of breads (or bread products like that last hot dog bun) and the last few bites of a plain cereal, and the last couple of crackers left in a box. It's a great way to use up the little bits and suddenly have tons of space in your cupboard and on top of your fridge!

Spread your bread out on a baking sheet. Bake for about 20 minutes at 350. Is it brittle? If yes, you've probably dried it enough, if not you want to dry it more. BUT be careful not to burn it, which can happen super quick. So if you're housecleaning and likely to be distracted, cook it longer at a lower temperature. You can also put the bread into a dehydrator.

Break the bread into small pieces with your fingers. You may want to place them in a large ziplock bag for the next step. Then, use your rolling pin, or a flat glass and roll those pieces into fine crumbs. You might or might not want to season them with some salt, pepper, and Italian seasoning.

Store in an airtight container.

Bananas go from Green to Brown in 2.2 days!

WHEN MY KIDS WERE LITTLE we used brown spotted bananas in smoothies every week.

Now I peel them, and freeze 2-3/bag to use later for banana bread, pancakes, or muffins. They will turn brown when frozen, but this does not affect the taste.

Sunday Soup

I TEND NOT TO DO THIS one very much, because my freezer space is too valuable, instead the chickens luck out. But you can save up many scraps through the week and then make soup once the container is full.

If you have simple leftovers, meat and veggies that may be seasoned but do not have a batter or breadcrumb coating, nor heavy sauce or cheese, you can turn them into soup. Simply collect them (and freeze as you go, so there is no spoilage) in a container. Then, add broth (see below) and simmer. Voila, soup! After it has thawed and simmered for an hour or so, taste it to decide what you need for herbs, salt, etc added. You may need to add onion, too. Mashed potatoes can work well to thicken a soup like this.

Vegetable Peels Are Stockable!

OK, TO BE FAIR I WOULD do this particular frugal trick only if you buy organic, at the farmers' market, or grow your own vegetables. To fully rinse off all the chemicals and waxes that are often on store-bought veggies is so difficult, that I would be afraid to do this with "regular-bought" produce.

Again in a container that you can store in the freezer until you are ready to use it, collect all the fresh (not dried/dead) leaves and peels from your veggies as you prepare your meals. Also, those 1-2 spoonfuls of leftover steamed or boiled vegetables go in the container rather than the compost.

When you have a containerful, dump it into a pot, cover with water and bring to a boil, then simmer a while (long enough for me to forget about it and then come back). Drain, saving the liquid back into the pot, adding the solids to your compost. Taste the liquid, your vegetable stock, and season it mildly with some herbs, salt, and pepper if you like. Or, wait until you use the stock to season it.

You can waterbath can this, but without knowing the acidity, I don't dare do this. Most likely it would be shelf-stable, but I'm not taking the chance. Instead, I jar it and save it in the fridge for a week or less. Use this for soups, crockpot liquid, for cooking rice, etc. You get the extra minerals from the vegetable waste you would have thrown out, more importantly you get the extra tastiness.

Better yet, after stripping a chicken carcass or beef bones, simmer your peels, those bones, and water to make a more flavorful stock. There is nothing quite as savory as homemade stock.

Thank you

Thank you so much for joining us for this book! We hope you found some new recipes to try and that they will become your favorites, too! Remember, start small, succeed, Expand!

Please consider signing up for our mailing list and follow us on social media to share ideas.

We would love it if you would leave us a testimonial or shout-out on social media! #SecondTimeAroundHomestead

Don't miss out!

Visit the website below and you can sign up to receive emails whenever Rachel Roy publishes a new book. There's no charge and no obligation.

https://books2read.com/r/B-A-EEVR-ZPGIC

BOOKS 2 READ

Connecting independent readers to independent writers.

About the Author

Rachel Roy lives in the Northeast Kingdom of Vermont with her husband and children. She has been writing for as long as she has known that people could create books. In 2021, her first children's story, Growing Up As Fairies, first appeared on Kindle Vella in serial format. After edits and illustrations she published it in print in December 2022. In the meantime she added six other series to Kindle Vella including another children's story, two non-fiction homesteading resources, and several fantasy and fantasy romances. Rachel also teaches middle school Humanities as she continues to write.

Read more at https://www.authorrachelroy.com.